John Boyd was born in 1912, the son of a locomotive engine driver
and was brought up in working-class east Belfast. He was educated
at 'Inst' (Royal Belfast Academical Institution), Queen's University, Belfast, and Trinity College Dublin. He has worked as a
teacher, lecturer and a BBC radio and television producer. On
retirement in 1972, he began a new career as a dramatist. Popular
success with his play *The Flats* was followed by the publication of
his *Collected Plays* Vols I and II by the Blackstaff Press. He is
currently an honorary director of the Lyric Theatre, Belfast, and
edits the literary magazine *Threshold*.

D1609999

OUT OF MY CLASS

-JOHN BOYD-

THE
BLACKSTAFF
PRESS
BELFAST AND DOVER, NEW HAMPSHIRE

Cover painting by Colin Middleton,
courtesy of Mr R.B. Jackson and with the permission
of Mrs K. Middleton

First published in 1985
by The Blackstaff Press
3 Galway Park, Dundonald, Belfast BT16 0AN, Northern Ireland
and
51 Washington Street, Dover, New Hampshire 03820 USA
with the assistance of
The Arts Council of Northern Ireland

Printed in Northern Ireland
by The Universities Press Limited

British Library Cataloguing in Publication Data

Boyd, John, 1912–
Out of my class.
1. Boyd, John, 1912– —Biography   2. Dramatists,
Irish—20th century —Biography
I. Title
822'.914   PR6052.0918/

Library of Congress Cataloging-in-Publication Data

Boyd, John, 1912–
Out of my class.
1. Boyd, John, 1912–   —Biography.   2. Dramatists,
Irish—20th century—Biography.   3. Belfast (Northern
Ireland) —Social life and customs.   I. Title.
PR6052.09185Z47   1985   822'.914   [B]   85–20016

ISBN 0 85640 337 7

CHAPTER ONE

Mother told me that I was born on the nineteenth of July in the early hours of the morning when everyone was asleep. When I asked her if she was asleep too she only laughed and shook her head. I didn't learn the answer to that question for a long time; it was something that mother didn't like to talk about. She once gave me a strange reply; 'Curiosity killed the cat,' she said in a serious tone of voice. I wondered why, because I was curious about everything myself and couldn't understand why a poor cat should be killed for doing no harm.

It was no good asking questions about how you came into the world because nobody seemed to know the right answer. Only one thing was sure: a lady called Mrs Glenfield was there at the time. She lived in Glenallen Street and brought me into the world, but how she did it nobody ever said. She was called a midwife and she found babies wherever she went. She found me. Mother said Mrs Glenfield was 'always on the go' after babies. Mrs Glenfield would pat my head when she saw me playing in the street and tell me I was growing up 'as straight as a rush'. But I didn't know what a rush was and a long time passed before I found out that rushes grew in fields, and there were no fields near our house. We lived in a city. It was called Belfast.

I was born in the heart of Ballymacarett, in number nine Baskin Street, off Templemore Avenue, between the Albert Bridge Road and the Newtownards Road. It was a small street of red-brick kitchen houses, and was the first home father and mother had after they were married. I was their first child. On my birth certificate father is described as 'Robert Boyd, Labourer' and mother as 'Jane Boyd, formerly Leeman'. There are also the words 'Agnes Glenfield present at birth'. My birth was registered on the fifth of August 1912.

Mother always said that father told a lie when he registered my birth: 'Your father had no right to call himself a labourer. When you were born he was a fireman on the railway. I'd never have married a common labourer, I can tell you that much!' But father argued that he used a shovel all day firing a locomotive on the Belfast and County Down Railway, and so had every right to call himself a labourer; even when he became an engine driver he still called himself a labourer; 'Luk at them hands o' mine,' he'd say. 'I've to use the scrubbin' brush t' git the dirt an' the grease aff them, haven't I?'

I don't remember living in the kitchen house where I was born, for after a couple of years we moved to another kitchen house in Bangor near the railway station. We lived there for only a couple of years as well, and father always said that these were the happiest years of his life, and that he wished he'd never been persuaded to leave Bangor. But mother was discontented there and wanted to go back to the dirt of Belfast; back to grandma Leeman and granda Leeman and all of her relations, such as the Herdmans, who lived on the Newtownards Road, opposite the big chapel whose name I didn't know because it was Roman Catholic and we were Protestants.

I've no memories of our Bangor house except that there was a small field at the back where I used to wander because I liked to feel the long grass on my legs and arms. But one day my aunt Ethel, father's sister, warned me, 'Don't go into that big field else you'll get lost. Or the gypsies'll come and take you away. You're like a wee gypsy, Topsy, aren't you?' Aunt Ethel always called me Topsy – a name I liked better than my real name, and I wished everybody would call me Topsy, but nobody else did. I think that was why aunt Ethel remained my favourite aunt. I should have liked to have been a gypsy boy living in a caravan and allowed to sit on the roundabouts all day, riding the horses that went up and down, and patting their wooden heads as if they were real horses, which they were, to me. But I was afraid of gypsies because they might snatch you away from the field one day and not let you home at night to lie in your bed.

I also remember walking along the sea wall holding tight my

2

father's hand. Sometimes he'd let my hand go and say, 'Careful now, walk by yourself.' But I was frightened that I might fall, for the wall was very high. Father would only laugh and tell me not to fear; that he wouldn't let me go, and anyway he was holding me at the back. Mother never played tricks like that. Whenever mother took hold of my hand she held it very tight and would never let it go, and then I could look at the sand and the sea without being afraid. I could trust mother not to let me go because she was my mother.

One morning a cart and a horse came to our door and took the furniture away. We returned to Ballymacarett and the rest of my childhood was spent there. Our house was number forty-six Chatsworth Street, a parlour house with a kitchen and scullery at the back, a back yard with a water closet, and two bedrooms upstairs. It was known as a 'respectable' street, and the musty parlour, which was seldom used except on Sundays, was a symbol of that respectability. Unfortunately number forty-six was at the Lord Street end. If our house had been at the Templemore Avenue end we would have been more comfortable, especially father who hardly ever got an unbroken day's sleep when he was on the nightshift; and when father was short of his sleep he was shorter still of temper, and even at the best of times his temper was short. The trouble was that father was a light sleeper, and the noises from the street would penetrate our front bedroom, wakening him up and sending him downstairs in his shirt and trousers and bare feet, his braces dangling down behind him.

'Jenny, for God's sake, tell them women across the street to shut up!'

'What's the matter, Bob?'

'I can't get my sleep!'

'Shut the window and you won't hear them.'

This suggestion always incensed father. 'Shut the winda! If I shut the winda how'll I get air? I've toul' ye before but ye won't niver listen t'me: if I shut the winda I feel suffocated! I'm used to fresh air, amn't I?'

'But if you're asleep. . .'

3

'I tell ye I can't get over asleep. An' I won't shut m'eyes if them 'uns across the way won't shut their traps!'

'They're only at their front doors talking. . .'

'Haven't they all housework t'do? Haven't they all houses to clean? God, but women have it easy!'

'They're only having a gossip. I can hardly go out and stop them, can I?'

'You were out gossipin' along wi' them!'

'I wasn't.'

'I heard ye, I heard ye, I know your voice, don't I?'

If we'd lived at the Templemore Avenue end father would have got a good day's sleep and, what was just as important, I'd have got peace to read and do my homework. But at the Lord Street end there was never any peace and quiet. Always neighbours gossiping, shouting and laughing; coal carts, milk carts, bread carts, carts of all kinds passing up and down; then, all day long, the out of work corner-boys in Lord Street playing football with a hanky ball, or playing a noisy game of marbles, or getting drunk on a Friday or Saturday night. Father said they were good for nothing, would neither work nor want and were always causing trouble. He told me not to go near them.

Now although our end of the street was the rowdy end I didn't mind the rowdiness all that much. At the kitchen table, where I did my homework, the noise disturbed me only because I was anxious to know what was going on outside. I was all for excitement – if a fight broke out in Lord Street I'd shut my exercise book and run outdoors without even bothering to let the ink dry or use my blotter. When this happened and my exercise was left unfinished or badly blotted it would be returned to me the next day with the word 'REJECTED' written across the page, and I'd be kept in after school to write the exercise all over again. Occasionally mother or father leafed through an old exercise book when it was finished and I needed a penny for a new one, and if the word 'REJECTED' shamed a page I'd be asked questions I couldn't answer. But usually I took care over my homework and always asked mother to back the exercise book with brown paper to keep it from harm. Five was the top mark and when father leafed through the book he'd say in a loud voice, 'Five, five, five, five! If you once can get five you can always get five!'

'That's asking too much, Bob!' mother said.

'Why?'

'Nobody can always be at their best.'

Father disagreed, but he knew all right what mother meant: she wasn't thinking of me but of herself when she made remarks like that.

'Four, four, three. . . another three. . . and another!'

'I told you, Bob –'

'REJECTED!'

It was hard for me to hold back my tears. I hated that word because it filled me full of shame.

What I can't understand is how I got the reputation for being clever. My aunt Ethel reiterated every time she saw me, 'There's more in that head of yours, Topsy, than the comb'll take out.' But I didn't really understand what she meant, though I was sure she meant it as a compliment. Aunt Ethel had the reputation of plastering people with compliments. As far as I was concerned this wasn't a fault but the opposite; I liked receiving compliments from grown-ups who liked giving me them, and after a while I got used to compliments and accepted them as my due. Anyway, for some reason I got this reputation for having brains and did my best to keep it by remaining quiet in the company of grown-ups. As a matter of fact I hadn't much to say to anyone who was older than myself. I preferred the company of the gang in our street to any visitor or relation who came to see us, and if I could slip out without being noticed I did so. Thinking of a plausible excuse was of course the difficulty, but sometimes a friend of mother's, in for a good gossip, would notice me sitting at the table reading, or pretending to read, and would say, 'Why don't you go out into the street?' And mother would add, 'You've read enough for one day. . . Away you go now.'

I was always a great one for reading and was supposed never to have my nose out of a book or a magazine. But I liked playing with our gang even more than I liked reading, so whenever I'd the choice of playing cowboys and Indians or having a quiet read on my own I'd no difficulty in making up my mind. I was a good runner and dodger and I loved games of chasing. But the disadvantage of playing cowboys and Indians was that because I was small for my age one of the bigger boys would command, 'You be the girl!' That was a role I hated: first of all, when you were caught and cornered, both sides would grab hold of you until you would have to yell, 'Let me go! Let me go!', and kick your way free; and secondly, I never imagined myself in any role other than the 'good 'un', that is, the hero, based on my favourite cowboy, Tom Mix.

Though I was certainly a glutton for books I was also a glutton for the 'pictures'. And the 'pictures' meant attending matinees in the 'New Princess', the 'Old Princess' and the 'Popular', three cinemas on the Newtownards Road. Of the three I'd a preference for the 'New Princess' which, we all agreed, had usually the most exciting 'pictures'. I don't think I even knew the word 'film' at that time, and of course the 'pictures' were long before the 'talkies'. The only kind of films that bored us were called romances; the love scenes between hero and heroine would arouse our derision, which we expressed by whistling loudly with two fingers stuck in our mouths.

I was between five and six when I was sent to the Ledley National School in Lord Street. It was thought to be a rough school and I stayed there for only a month or two until mother succeeded in getting me a place in Mountpottinger National School, which was regarded as the best national school in the whole of Bally-macarett. I remember hardly anything about the infants class at the Ledley, except that we sat on very low, well-worn wooden forms, and that when we stood up there were always wet patches where we'd sat. I also remember that we used slates to write our letters of the alphabet, and that we'd wipe them clean at the end of school with little damp sponges. Our teacher was very tiny compared with other grown-ups. She was kind and never scolded any of us, so when I was told that I would be sent to Mountpottinger I wasn't at all pleased. But I didn't say a word; mother knew best and was always right.

It was through mother's boldness that I got placed in my new school. Although father was anxious that I should have the best schooling possible, he left the responsibility of my schooling to mother, simply because she was full of confidence in the presence of strangers and, according to father, was blessed with the 'gift of the gab' while he, faced with a clergyman, teacher or doctor, became tongue-tied and foolish.

Mother was very small. She always maintained she was just over five foot, but father wouldn't allow her even that height and would say to me, 'Come on boy, get your ruler out o' your bag an' we'll measure your mother's exact height.' Mother would protest that it was silly to measure her height when she knew perfectly well what it was; but father's will would prevail and mother, with a placatory sigh, would give way to his whim, throwing at me a conspiratorial look as if to say, 'That's your father all over, trying to make me out smaller than I am.' So the three of us would leave the kitchen (mother wouldn't permit pencil marks on the good wallpaper) and she'd stand straight up against the scullery wall while father carefully measured her, closing one eye to make certain that the ruler was exactly horizontal before making his pencil mark.

'Well, Bob, what height am I?'

'I make you five foot and a quarter inch!'

'Well, didn't I tell you that's what I was!'

'I didn't think you were, Jenny, honest I didn't.'

'You believe me now then, don't you?'

But father, scientifically-minded as he was in such matters, wasn't so easily convinced.

'You measure now, boy, to make doubly sure,' and he'd hand me over ruler and pencil, and I'd stand on a kitchen chair and take the measurements, obeying his command to keep the ruler dead straight. 'Let me see from here.' Father would stand back a yard or so – he couldn't go back much further in our scullery – and then, having got a better perspective, would suddenly give a howl, but not one of his angry howls.

'You haven't your shoes off! You haven't them off, that's what's wrong! You done that on purpose, Jenny, to cod me!'

7

Mother would then be persuaded to take off her shoes and be measured again, and again father would be tricked; for mother would stand on her tiptoes, putting her forefinger up to her lips to make me a conspirator. Again father's measurement – which he was careful to define as 'approximate', a word he was proud of – came to just over five foot; this always amazed him, he measured mother at least once a year and knew her to be under five foot. 'There's something wrong about this. That oul' floor's uneven, isn't it?'

Eventually mother, tired of playing her tricks, would confess to standing on her tiptoes and agree to be properly measured. She was four foot ten and a half inches, just the same as last year. Then I'd be asked to measure father himself, after the usual command to keep the ruler dead straight, and father's height wouldn't have changed from last year either; five foot ten and a half inches. 'Just approximately a foot higher nor you, girl.' Whenever father called mother 'girl' I knew he was in good form and pleased with her, because whenever he was in bad form he'd call mother other names, names that made me want to cover my ears so as not to hear.

At the end of the measuring father would pick up mother's shoes to examine them. 'They're all over in the heels. . . they're in a bad state. . . you shouldn't be wearin' them at all. . . they're done. . . look, they're lettin' in. . . yer feet must be gettin' wet.'

Father was meticulous about his own footwear; he'd a pair of what he called his 'railway' boots, a pair of 'weekday' boots and a pair of 'Sunday' boots. All three pairs he kept well-polished, taking most care with his Sunday boots, which he'd spend half an hour over on a Saturday, sitting on the sofa in the kitchen, the boots on top of an old *Belfast Telegraph* or *Empire News* which was spread on the floor.

Although a regular churchgoer all his life – we were lapsed Presbyterians turned Congregationalists – father never opened his Bible from one Sunday to the next, except in church and even there he hardly bothered to follow the readings, preferring to concentrate on the sermon, but only if it was a lively one; otherwise he'd gaze round the church, noting who was present.

'I didn't notice the Reids there this mornin',' he'd say to mother as they were walking home along the Albert Bridge Road. 'Did you?'

'No, Bob, I wasn't looking for them.'

'They weren't in their pew.'

'Weren't they? I never noticed.'

'There's usually some one of the Reids in their pew.'

'I never notice such things.'

I liked walking to church on Sunday morning, father holding one hand, mother the other, for this was the only time in the whole week that the three of us looked our best: father wearing his well-brushed navy-blue suit and soft hat; mother her newest coat and hat, and shoes that met with father's approval; and myself with a fresh jersey and stockings with coloured turned-down tops held up by comfortable black elastic garters. But though I enjoyed walking to and from church I always thought the service itself, which lasted from half past eleven to about a quarter to one, far too long. I liked the singing of the hymns best of all, though mother often complained, sometimes lightly and sometimes seriously, that father sang much too loud and was always out of tune – so much so that the worshippers in the row in front would turn their heads to the right or left as a token gesture of reproach. Mother had a sweet soprano voice – before her marriage she'd sung in her church choir – and many a time she tugged at father's sleeve and whispered something to him. But in vain; father refused to be denied his pleasure. During the prayers or, what was worse, during the sermon itself, he had a habit of yawning and forgetting to put his hand to his mouth so, as I sat between them, mother would bend over and whisper, 'Tell your father it's bad manners to yawn,' and when I tugged at his sleeve and delivered the message he'd nod acknowledgment of his misdeed and reply, 'I'm that sleepy I can't help it.' Then mother would deliver another message, 'Tell him that's no excuse,' and in defiance of that, father would silently mouth, 'Shut up, you!'

CHAPTER TWO

Father was a well-built, upstanding man who held his head high as he strode along the street, swinging his arms. I remember that neighbours used to comment on his looks. 'Your Bob's a fine lukkin' man, Jenny. You're the luckiest woman in the whole of the street. Your husband's niver out o' work. Niver breaks your pay. Niver puts his foot inside the door of a pub.' Father prided himself on his appearance whether going to work or church, or just taking a stroll round the town on a Saturday evening. Driving a loco-motive was a dirty job, he constantly maintained, but that was no reason for slovenliness; so, before leaving the house for work he would take a final check of himself to make sure everything was right from top to toe. The brass sign on his railway cap – BCDR – had to be shining and the cap itself rubbed clean with the bit of waste he always carried in one of his pockets. His railway jacket had to be well-brushed and the brass buttons given a rub. His dungarees had to be as clean as could be, and their condition was discussed almost daily, mother protesting that it was impossible to get rid of all the stains of oil and dirt, and father arguing that other drivers' wives were able to wash dungarees to make them look like new. Finally, he'd check that the laces of his boots wouldn't let him down, and after easing on each boot he'd give the lace a strong tug to test its reliability.

'What pieces have you give me?'

'I made you cheese ones. You like cheese, don't you?'

'Yes, but I'd cheese yesterday, hadn't I?'

'I can't remember what I put in your pieces yesterday.'

'If you'd to ate them you'd mind what was in them.'

'Ach, I've more important things than that to think about.'

'Oh, you've more important things to think about? What have you to think about, eh?'

As likely as not, father would unwrap the newspaper round his two pieces – one for each jacket pocket – and examine what mother had given him. He was nearly always dissatisfied. Either the bread wasn't fresh enough or else it was cut far too thick. Mother would protest, 'But how can you cut fresh bread thin? It can't be done, Bob!'

Then father might lose his temper, shout, and smack the table.

'Why don't you make up pieces the way I want them?'

'I don't know how you want them, Bob!'

I could easily have told mother how father liked to have his pieces made up, for his taste in sandwiches was just the same as my own, but of course I kept quiet at such times; and when both of them would disappear into the scullery to make up the pieces again, I'd slip out into the street. It was best to be out of the way at such times.

I had plenty of chums and usually one or two would be out playing. Somehow our street was never dull. I liked to sit on our parlour window-sill and read comics like *Chips* and *Comic Cuts* or boys' weeklies like *Rover, Adventure, Magnet* or *Gem*. I was, I suppose, the greediest reader in our street, for as soon as I had read my comics and boys' weeklies I would hide them away in bundles for re-reading. I must have thought then, as I still think, that a good story improves on re-reading. But though I preferred fiction, I also read for information, which was one of the reasons why I collected cigarette cards. It was from this source I learnt that Chatsworth Street was named after a Great House somewhere in England. What possible connection there could be between our narrow street and a palatial building like Chatsworth House completely defeated me, but I was glad to discover that the name Chatsworth – which I never cared for – had some grand connection. I didn't know anything about 'poor relations' then, but if I had I expect I would have put our street in that category.

Whenever I came out to read, one of my chums would eventually join me: Hugh McClune, whose father was a tram-driver, a much more humdrum job than father's; Norman McIlroy, whose father worked in an engineering firm; and Tom Prichard, an only child whose father I can't remember at all. Strangely enough, nearly all the children of my own age lived at our end, the lower end of the street. The only exception was the Sinnerton family who, to my great relief, lived at the top end. I feared all three of the boys – all had closely cropped hair, protruding teeth, and a reputation for using their feet in a fight. If I was sent on a message in the direction of Templemore Avenue – perhaps to the Co-op grocery – which would involve having to pass their door and run the risk of meeting them, I'd make a detour in the interest of personal safety. I was fond of what we called 'scrapping' though, and often engaged in contests for fun with open hands so that no damage could be inflicted. But I avoided fist fights in earnest as they could result in bloody noses and black eyes. Physically I was timid and a great coward: imaginatively I wallowed in extraordinary deeds of daring; and the exciting stories in *Rover* and *Adventure* provided me with plenty of material to identify with. Unfortunately I couldn't come up to my heroes in real life.

Though I couldn't bear to be hurt, I'd a reckless, exhibitionistic streak which made me show off in front of our gang. For instance, because I'd a good head for heights I enjoyed climbing backyard walls and standing on top of them with arms outstretched, then walking precariously along. From this height and vantage I could peer into neighbours' kitchens until I was spotted and fists were shaken so that I would have to jump off the wall and scamper up the narrow back entry to the safety of the street. However, my most reckless exploit – I was about nine at the time – occurred during a walk to the Victoria Park which was roughly a mile away. An old ricketty wooden bridge led to the park, but instead of crossing the bridge in the ordinary way, I was 'dared' to cross on the outside of the wooden paling. I made the crossing with extreme caution, the green smelly ooze of the Connswater river far beneath, and the fear that if I stumbled and fell I would be sucked down into the slime and never be seen again. I reached the other side triumphantly.

When we visited the Victoria Park on a hot summer day we always made straight for the pond called the Sucker, which was reputed not to be very deep, but I never had enough courage to test

12

that. I was able to swim across it before I was ten, having quickly learnt to swim in the Templemore Avenue baths. All of us loved swimming in the Sucker – the very name suggested a dangerous death-dealing adventure – and the Sucker had many advantages over the baths: it was free; we could swim naked and dry ourselves by running about and playing chasing games in the long grass all round the pond; and we never, of course, mentioned these exploits to our parents!

But once – I may as well record it now though it happened years later – the Sucker was almost the scene of a drowning. I was in the company of two or three others from our street, and on this afternoon was supposed to be in charge of my younger brother Jim, then only about three years old. Normally I wouldn't have thought of taking him so far from home, but this was a hot summer day and I was persuaded – not that I needed much persuasion – to let him accompany our little gang, everyone agreeing to take a turn in carrying Jim on his back. We reached the pond, had our swim and then began running about. Suddenly I noticed that Jim had disappeared, and when I ran back to the pond I discovered that he'd fallen in and was lying head downwards so that I could see only the back of his woolly green jersey. Luckily he was about a yard or so from the edge, but even that meant he was floating in about two feet of water. For a moment I thought he had been drowned, for I didn't know how long he'd been there. I dragged him out and laid him on the grass. His eyes were open and he wasn't even scared; he told me he'd just been looking into the water. So we took off his clothes, which soon dried in the hot sun, and none of us ever mentioned what had happened.

On sunny days Victoria Park attracted us like a magnet, but even when the weather was dull we would often desert our street and neighbourhood and make our way there. For years I'd an obsession with little yachts and got endless pleasure from them, especially sailing them across the Sucker. I bought my first one in Anderson's shop at the top of Templemore Avenue. It was a very small shop, but I never saw a shop crammed with so many toys in the window and in shelves up to the ceiling. A visit to Anderson's was for me a view of paradise.

The purchase of my first yacht proved a disaster. It was red with lovely white, starchy sails. I brought it home and put it in the small oval zinc bath which mother used for washing clothes. It looked magnificent in the water, though it could move only about six inches, but that didn't matter much. For a long time I was content just to gaze on it lovingly and imagine the voyages it might make. But at last I grew weary of my yacht becalmed in a zinc bath in our backyard and decided it must prove itself by a voyage across the Sucker. I chose a windy day and went alone, loth to share the pleasure of its maiden voyage with anyone else. I pushed the yacht into the choppy waves and it sailed gloriously away into the middle of the pond where it had to contend with even choppier waves. There it fell on its side and I'd the choice of leaving it to its fate or swimming out to retrieve it. I retrieved it and brought it home. But I never put it in the zinc bath again, never brought it to the Sucker again, and it lay neglected in the backyard for a long while, until one night father accidentally trampled on it and I threw it into the bin in disgust.

I decided to ask father's advice about my next yacht. He told me a yacht must have a heavy keel: that was the most important part, and of course the part I hadn't even thought of. So he brought me to a toyshop in town and selected a much smaller yacht, but with a good keel. Though I was disappointed by the size of my new yacht and the smallness of its sail, I was overjoyed when I discovered it could skim across the Sucker on the windiest of days, the huge waves unable to topple it over on its side. When I told father of its successful maiden voyage he inclined his head and said knowingly, 'Well, boy, that's learnt you somethin', hasn't it?' It had, but I wasn't quite sure what. Father had a habit of making remarks that I couldn't make sense of.

Unless the weather was very bad, I preferred to be out of doors than indoors. This was because in our street things were always happening. Indoors nothing exciting ever took place except a quarrel between father and mother, and that was something I found so disturbing that I'd have done almost anything to avoid it. These quarrels would keep me outside even on a drizzly day.

Chatsworth Street was noisy when traffic was passing up and down; the street was cobbled with what we called 'pavers', and the noise created by the iron-rimmed wheels of the carts and vans would make the windows shake. We youngsters kept a sharp look-out for vans that we could 'hop' – that is, we'd let them pass without taking any apparent notice of them, then we'd crouch double, race after them, and hop on the back without being noticed. Sometimes we'd get hops as far as the Castlereagh or Bloomfield Road without being detected, then we'd jump off with a shout of triumph which would make the driver turn round and shake his whip at us. Some drivers were furious at being tricked into giving us a free ride; others were amused and didn't seem to mind our company at all; they would let us stay on board until we tired of the bumpy ride and began thinking of our long walk home.

When the 'slummage' carts with their horrible smell appeared in the street we held our noses and pretended to vomit. I was told that slummage was what was left over when whiskey was manu-factured, and I could well believe that. Anyway, I detested the sight and smell of it; for it reminded me of the sour smell from the two public-houses in Lord Street, one in front of our house, and the other at the back, both with swinging doors that when opened gave off a stench that always made me wrinkle up my nose. As bad as the slummage carts were the carts that collected refuse: these were small grimy affairs, with a sad donkey or mule between the shafts. I liked the dirty coal carts because of the big patient horses that would let you approach so close that you could count the hairs on their noses; some were so friendly that they let you caress them. I also liked to watch the grimy-faced coal men, hoisting their big black lumpy bags onto their backs and tramping up our hallway into the kitchen, then throwing off their loads, amid a cloud of dust, into our coal hole.

When mother bought milk from Willie Catherwood, our milk-man, whose fair wavy hair I envied, I liked to stand on the step of his cart to watch the milk gush from one of the two big cans – the other contained buttermilk – and when our jug was full, mother, knowing what was in my mind, would say, 'You look thirsty.

Want a drink?' Of course I wanted a drink; but even more I wanted a ride in Willie's cart. Sometimes he would say, 'Jump up, lad, an' houl' on tight', but at other times – I suppose when he was in a hurry – he'd ignore me and say, 'Gee up. . . Gee up there' to his horse and proceed to the top of the street.

Bread servers never gave lifts. Nevertheless when ours appeared – we belonged to the Co-op – I would hang around the cart until the server shouted to me: 'Tell your mother bread.' And when I returned with her I stood by her side, not only because I loved the smells of the bread – white and brown loaves, baps and currants, wheaten, sodas and potato – but because mother didn't need to ask me what was in my mind. She knew I wanted a bun, and I don't remember her ever refusing me my choice, which could be a custard, an apple, or a jam bun. Sometimes, very often in fact, she'd send me indoors with a white loaf while she crossed the street for a gossip with Mrs McClune or Mrs McIlroy. I'd place the loaf carefully on the kitchen table and stand for a moment uncertain whether or not to yield to temptation. I always yielded. The flaky skin of a fresh white loaf was irresistible, even though I'd only just devoured my bun. The problem was how much loaf I could safely nibble at without getting into trouble. Sometimes my theft was noticed, sometimes not; but mother would often keep me out of temptation's way by taking the loaf with her as she crossed the street for one of her long neighbourly gossips.

During a hot spell in the summer the corporation water cart would come round the streets, and usually before it appeared in our street the rumour would have spread that it was on its way, perhaps already in Thorndyke Street or Paxton Street. As soon as this good news was heard, our gang would get ready for action. If we weren't in our bare feet – and in summer we often were – we'd stuff our stockings inside our boots for safety, hide them behind the hall door, hitch up our short trousers as high as they'd go, and wait for the water man to appear. Then, with shouts of delight we'd follow after the cart, the cool jets playing over our legs and feet.

Though I loved reading and could sit for hours over boys'

magazines – and a few years later devoured the books I borrowed from Templemore Avenue public library – I was even keener on games. We played football in the street, but always had to be on the look-out for a policeman who might, when least expected, appear in Lord Street and then we'd have to run towards Templemore Avenue, heart-scared that another would appear there and we'd be cornered and captured. What would have happened to us then we didn't dare to imagine. Naturally, I have retained a mistrust of the police ever since.

Between our street and Constance Street lay a small gritty patch of ground which we also used for playing football, cricket and rounders. We called this patch the 'wee field', though its resemblance to a grassy field was remote. Our 'wee field', however, was our precious possession because although muddy and full of puddles in wet weather, it at least provided us with an open space. Here too we were frightened of being caught and arrested by the police. Still, despite the mud and the unevenness of the ground, we made it into a miniature playing pitch, and it had the added advantage of having no windows close at hand; for whenever a parlour window was broken during a street game there'd be a wild argument over who was responsible and who'd have to fork out the money. Usually rough justice was done and the parents of all the miscreants would share the cost of the broken pane.

Lord Street marked the boundary between the 'respectable' parlour houses such as ours, and the slummy kitchen houses of Constance Street and the even more slummy Edith Street, known as 'The Gut'. In these streets many of the women wore brown or black shawls round their shoulders, and the men – most of them permanently out of work – slouched in and out of the pubs or stood chatting at the gable walls in their duncher caps, with mufflers instead of collars and ties, and shabby jackets with tattered worn sleeves. The younger men played game after game of marbles, called 'bulking', in the middle of the road, or in the 'wee field' when the ground was dry. On Fridays and Saturdays these corner-boys, as father called them, disappeared into the two pubs and only reappeared at closing time, sometimes so drunk they could hardly stagger out; then they would lie stretched on the pavement in front of the pubs and bawl out songs such as 'Nellie Dean' and 'I'll be your sweetheart' when they were in sentimental mood, or Orange ballads such as 'The Orange Lily O!' when they were feeling aggressive; and their aggressiveness often ended in a street fight. Fists and feet would fly and women would join in, with screams of rage, to protect their men, and the police would arrive – usually after the violence had been quelled. These fights I wasn't allowed to witness at close quarters. As soon as one broke out I'd be called indoors, and would stand with my nose pressed against our parlour window, my heart thumping with fear when a head was bashed against a wall.

This corner, bisected by Lord Street, centred on the 'wee field', Constance Street, and our end of Chatsworth Street. According to father, it was the worst spot in the whole of Ballymacarett, with its pubs, a bookie's office, an almost derelict shop which had once been a spirit grocer's, and Pilsen's shop, which displayed a crime magazine called *Police News* in its window. Pilsen's had an acrid smell so powerful that I would try not to breathe in when I was buying a poke of sweets for myself, or a packet of cigarettes for my father.

At the corner of the 'wee field' stood a relic of the past: a four-sided pole, painted red, white and blue, seven feet high, and remarkable for its festoonery of cast-off horseshoes from top to bottom. It was an enticement for natural climbers like myself who, faced with such a challenge, had to accept it, and view the length of Lord Street from its height. Our horseshoe pole memorialized the site of a smithy, but I remained ignorant of this morsel of local history until many years after I'd left Chatsworth Street. Besides being a colourful memorial, especially in July when it was freshly painted and given a halo of small Union Jacks, our pole was regarded as the private property of the corner-boys who lounged daily round it and who never failed to produce a collecting-box early in June for the ostensible purpose of re-decoration, but in fact to provide them with drinking money for the summer months.

The gable wall of the pub at the side of the 'wee field' had the

18

ubiquitous painting of King William of Orange crossing the Boyne. It was the first work of art I ever saw, and I've seen it so often since – on Orange banners during the Twelfth of July procession and on dozens of street walls in Belfast – that I now loathe the sight of it. But once I was fascinated by it, and wondered what it all meant: the proud king with sword on high; the gallant steed on which he sat so upright and unafraid; and the green grassy slopes of the river Boyne in the background. I didn't know where the Boyne was, except that it was somewhere in Ireland, and I didn't know anything about King William the Third except that he led the Protestants against the Catholics at the Battle of the Boyne and beat them – a victory all Protestants were proud of, though nobody, except my granda Leeman, could tell me why: when I asked him, his answer was so tersely authoritative that I accepted it as gospel truth:

'He saved us from Popery!'

To save us Protestants from Popery was unquestionably a good thing, so my naturally inquiring mind was satisfied – at least for the time being.

Granda Leeman was an Orange man and paraded every Twelfth of July with his lodge to the field where the bands and lodges all gathered to listen to speeches. He was a stalwart Protestant, no doubt about that. The curious fact about him – and grandma Leeman too – was that they hardly ever attended church. And that I couldn't understand. But it was only one of the many puzzles that agitated my mind. If curiosity killed the cat, as mother said it did, then I had to learn to curb my own curiosity, otherwise I'd have a very short life indeed.

CHAPTER THREE

When mother secured me a place in Mountpottinger National School she was instrumental in putting my foot on the first rung of the educational ladder: if I hadn't attended this school my entire education would have been different.

It was as a result of topographical chance – as well as on mother's initiative – that I was given a place. Mother must have impressed the principal – Mr McKee – with her appearance and her eagerness to give me a good start in life; and it was the general opinion in Ballymacarett that – with the exception of the Model schools somewhere on the other side of the city – Mountpottinger was the best school in Belfast for a working-class boy or girl whose parents had ambitions for their offspring.

The school was about a hundred yards from the top of our street, which meant that I could reach it in a minute or so if I walked. But I never walked; I ran in the mornings out of fear of being late, for if you were late and missed the bell – rung by the principal himself standing magisterially at the top of the wooden staircase – you would be caned on the hand or given half an hour's detention after school. And I would run home at full pelt when the last class was dismissed. I'd gallop with my bag tucked under one arm – for I wouldn't take the time to sling it across my shoulders – and my navy cap, with its entwined lettering MS, stuffed in my other hand. I'd feel great, breathing in the fresh air after the stuffiness of the classrooms.

I covered this short distance between home and school for about six years, four times a day, and I don't believe I ever grew tired of it; it was too full of interest. I seldom ran home without stopping at least once, usually at Jane Snell's confectionery shop for the pleasure of looking at the bottles of sweets, caramels, boilings, liquorice, chocolates. This shop window was as drably dressed as its owner, whom we derisively nicknamed 'Jane Stink', shouting the insulting sobriquet every time we caught sight of her at the counter, a disgruntled look on her swarthy face. None of us ever gave her our custom except on the rare occasions when her shop was open and every other one shut, and even then I didn't dare to face her: she might recognise me as one of the miscreants. 'Be sure your sins will find you out' was printed outside the Iron Mission Hall just a few yards from her shop and I took that for a warning.

Almost anything could halt my headlong dash home in the afternoons: the open door of the Presbyterian church adjacent to the school – I liked to peep in, though such curiosity was strictly forbidden; the pillars and shallow steps of the Orange Hall on the Albert Bridge Road – I liked to encircle the pillars and play at jumps from the steps; the large beautifully-shaped bottles in Wilson's chemist shop, full of red and blue liquid which I imagined would be lovely to taste, the colours so crystal clear. Then there were the passing red trams destined for Castle Junction in the middle of the city, or for Dundonald graveyard at the end of the lines. If you carefully placed two or three nails on the lines and waited until a tram came lurching along and ran over them, what a surprise! Each nail – no matter how rusty – would be transformed into a miniature silver sword, and would be still warm when you rushed forward to pick it up after the flattening. And a tram could sometimes be hopped when the conductor was upstairs, and if you were lucky you could hold on for the whole length of a stop. But I seldom hopped trams on my way home from school for fear of losing my schoolbag.

Our school, hidden behind the Presbyterian church at the top of Paulett Avenue, was invisible from the main Albert Bridge Road. In front of the two-storied red-brick building lay a triangular playground, flanked by a high red-brick wall; and all day long, before lessons began and after they ended, the hum of machinery floated over that wall; but nobody ever told us what was made in the factory, and I didn't discover until long after I'd left school that ventilating fans were manufactured there and sent all over the world, especially to India. Curious that our teachers kept this a secret. Maybe they didn't know themselves, but that was unlikely, because a lot of geography was taught and we knew all the counties, rivers and headlands of Ireland off by heart; and along the dark green walls large faded maps were hung up high for everyone to look at all day, so that a teacher, armed with a long pole, could point out places anywhere in the world. We were told the world was round like a globe, or, more accurately, like an orange, because it was squashed at both ends, the north pole where the Arctic Ocean was, and the south pole where the Antarctic Ocean was. One of my early ambitions was to be the first explorer in the world to reach both poles on a sleigh, with husky dogs barking all the way to keep me company, or with reindeer who would be better company still.

In Mountpottinger boys and girls were strictly segregated and I was hardly aware of the girls' school beneath us on the ground floor; we arrived at and left school at slightly different times, and I don't remember ever once speaking to a girl. Anyway, as I wasn't much interested in girls either at school or in the street, I regarded our segregation as right and proper. Occasionally we saw them skipping in their part of the playground, but as that territory was forbidden to us we took little notice of them. The only time we were conscious of their presence was when during our lessons the silence was broken by their shrill voices singing songs like 'Annie Laurie', 'Oft in the stilly night' or 'The Minstrel Boy'. We thought our own singing far superior to theirs.

From the very beginning our principal impressed on us that we were privileged to belong to Mountpottinger. Ours wasn't an ordinary school and we must never forget that. We were there to work hard and to do our very best for ourselves, our parents and our school. We were there to learn the 3 R's – reading, 'riting and 'rithmetic – and all our teachers were there to give us a 'good grounding' that would last us all our lives. Such was the sum and substance of the homilies delivered by Mr McKee during the half-hour change of classrooms, when he stood on a stool and made us march in step to the tink. . . tink. . . tink of a tiny bell half hidden in his hand. These class changes were conducted in a military fashion, each of us gazing steadily at the nape of the boy

22

in front, and taking extreme care not only to march in strict time to the bell but also to keep the right distance from the boy in front until we filed into a classroom or were conducted round the ring in the big room and ordered to halt. These changes relieved the monotony of our lessons, allowed us to stretch our legs, and gave us the chance to whisper a few words without moving our lips. If we had ambitions to become ventriloquists – and I *had* – these half-hour changes would certainly have given us practice. In any event, they gave Mr McKee the chance to reiterate his little homilies. It never once entered my head to doubt their truth as guides towards a virtuous and successful life.

Indeed I seldom doubted the word of any adult, and certainly never dreamt of disputing the word of a teacher. Adults were old and wise, and therefore truthful; boys were young and foolish, and therefore told lies. But even a boy didn't tell lies for the sake of lying: he told lies for very good reasons – to keep out of trouble. And if a lie kept you out of trouble it was called a fib, and a fib did nobody any harm. That is, if it was successful. If it wasn't successful it turned into a lie, and therefore made you a liar. Our school turned me into an unrepentant cheat and liar. Life without cheating and lying was impossible for deceit was necessary to prevent punishment. Talking during lessons was forbidden, for example, but when a teacher turned his back on the class to write on the blackboard, some boy might occasionally be bold enough to whisper a few words to a neighbour.

'Who's doing the talking?'
Nobody would admit.
'Those doing the talking put up their hands!'
No hands were put up.
'I repeat: those who were talking put up their right hands!'
No hands were put up.
'In that case, the whole class will be kept in after school!'
Despair would descend on us all – and a feeling of injustice as well. Everybody was going to be punished because two or three boys were too frightened to put up their hands and admit they were the guilty ones. Then the inquisition would follow:
'Did anybody *see* anybody talking?' Silence. A long silence. No

23

movement at first. Then a turning of heads.

'Nobody saw anybody talking? Nobody?'

Silence. A long silence. Then a single hand would go up, slowly and not very far. And the culprits would be pointed at, and they would deny the charge, and the rest of the class would deny the denial. Then the cane, hidden behind the blackboard, would be produced – a long, slightly bent yellow cane which the teacher would caress from one end to the other before it was so tightly gripped that his knuckles would turn white.

'Hold out your hand! Come on, open it out!'

And the swish followed, and the wounded hand was dishonoured with a welt, then hidden away for shame under the armpit of the other arm.

I was frightened of the cane, and the lessons I most feared were those when our class was arranged in a semi-circle in the big room, that is, the main room where four large classes were taught, so that it would be difficult to concentrate on your own class. We were usually taught arithmetic and spelling round the ring, as we called it. I was good at spelling and enjoyed putting a tick after each correctly spelt word so that I might then be proud of a ladder of ticks from the top to the bottom of my page without having an ugly line drawn through a misspelt word or a correct spelling repeated three or six or twelve times, according to the teacher's whim. But the half-hour spent doing our sums was an ordeal which haunts me even now. When I try to recall what my schooldays were like it is this half-hour that springs first to my mind: a half-hour of terror and dismay which seemed to last so long that it appeared to me to be interminable. This was the first time I realised the relativity of time: happiness passed quickly, but with terror time came to a stop. Though I was good at arithmetic, I often became so nervous and tense whenever our class was standing round the ring that I would shiver and be unable to do even the simplest sums.

A sum would be chalked up on the blackboard and we'd copy it into our jotters. Sometimes I was guilty of copying it incorrectly so that the sum was bound to come out wrong. We would then be ordered to take a right turn so that we'd be in a back-to-back position, which made any cogging very hard indeed. Nevertheless, when the teacher's attention was transferred to the black-board, some of us would snatch a quick look at the answer arrived at by the boy in front. If this coincided with our own answer – joy; if it didn't – doubt. Then came the command 'left turn', and we would face the teacher with our jotters on display. The right answer would then be announced and those who got it wrong would have to hold out their right hand to be slapped. So, in the course of half an hour – if you were unlucky or careless or poor at sums or almost paralysed with fear – you might receive more than half a dozen slaps. If you had already been given two or three on the right hand the teacher would shout, 'Other hand' and you'd present your uninjured left hand. Sometimes I marched away with two red swollen stinging hands which I would hide under my armpits for comfort.

Do I exaggerate the terror endured during these lessons, and the pain of the slaps inflicted on us? All I'm certain of is that this is one of the childhood terrors that cannot be erased from my memory. But I'm equally certain that not all our teachers were tyrants, and that some treated us with kindliness and humour – especially the women teachers of the junior classes. The truth is that the conditions were abominable and made good teaching impossible: we were herded into classes of fifty, perhaps more, and shunted about the school like automatons; and we were taught like automatons too, so that our imaginations were discouraged. But if our imaginations were discouraged they were not deadened: children are tough creatures and have a remarkable capacity for endurance and survival, physically and psychically. And our school wasn't all tyranny and fear, for I certainly enjoyed the reading, writing, drawing and singing classes.

I cannot recall the 'readers' we were given in the junior classes, but the books we studied from the age of ten still remain vividly in my mind – even the colour of their bindings. First of all, but not most important: *Julius Caesar* and *The Merchant of Venice*. I am not convinced that Shakespeare *should* be taught at an early age – there are strong arguments for and against it. But what I *am* absolutely sure of is that his plays should not have been taught to us as they were. To begin with, none of us had ever been in a theatre.

25

We'd never seen a play professionally performed, and we'd never even seen a play performed by amateurs. Yet here we were, children of nine or ten, being introduced to great plays with complex themes and characters, written in a language and style completely unfamiliar to us. In addition to these formidable obstacles, we had to study the texts while huddled in wooden forms, a teacher bellowing out long, largely incomprehensible speeches. The miracle is – and it is Shakespeare's – that *something* was somehow communicated to us: the murder of Caesar, the manliness of Brutus, the slyness of Cassius, the craftiness of Shylock, the cleverness of Portia, the suspense of the three caskets. Altogether, an introduction to interesting characters and exciting stories. So, as far as I was concerned, Shakespeare was worthwhile even then. But only just; for pleasure was mixed with pain.

I thought *Kidnapped* by Robert Louis Stevenson more enjoyable than a play by William Shakespeare: I brought *Kidnapped* home, asked mother to put a nice brown paper back on it, wrote my name and class and school, in my best handwriting, and immediately began the story. I had it finished almost before our reading aloud in class had begun. I'd never have accomplished that with *Julius Caesar* or *The Merchant of Venice*. For sheer enjoyment *Kidnapped* was a clear winner, as was *The Heroes* by Charles Kingsley, especially the tale of Jason's quest for the golden fleece. And for utter boredom nothing could have equalled a thick red-backed volume with some such title as 'Life in a Pond'. I never waded through even a single page of this turgid stuff, and I remember we had to give up reading it aloud in class.

This was the extent of my formal reading when the time came for me to leave Mountpottinger.

Luckily, when I was about nine, I learnt that you were allowed to borrow one book at a time from Ballymacarett public library in Templemore Avenue, keep it for a fortnight without being fined a penny (I was never fined) and you could even change it the day after you'd borrowed it – this I sometimes did, either because the book didn't appeal to me or because its appeal was so great that I finished it within a couple of hours.

A lesson in handwriting, or 'penmanship' as we were taught to dignify it, was an oasis in the school time-table. Our school was famous for its penmanship – famous, according to Mr McKee, not only in Ireland but throughout the entire world. His claim, I now think, may have been a little bit extravagant, but if it was, I would certainly exonerate him; all our teachers took inordinate pains to make us perfect clerks, and if there had been any justice in the world every Mountpottinger pupil would have been granted a stool in a comfortable office. I never had any ambition to be a clerk, but I don't consider the time and care we spent on hand-writing as entirely wasted. We were *drilled* to write well: first we were ordered to sit up straight; then told how to hold a pen properly, with forefinger straight, thumb well bent, the rest of the hand comfortably placed against the page; the left elbow had to be close to your side, left hand with fingers outstretched and together to hold the page firm; then the nib was dipped into the inkwell, carefully, and not too deep. No detail was left to chance. Consequently our Vere Foster copperplate style was remarkably similar – and totally without individuality.

I enjoyed our drawing classes though perhaps not for the right reasons; my main reason was that during them I experienced a wonderful sensation of relief and relaxation. Fear was absent: the cane was put away behind the blackboard, and a feeling of peace would permeate the whole class. But I did enjoy drawing and painting, and at home I spent hours at the kitchen table with my small box of paints. In particular, I was a tireless painter of ships – both steam and sailing – and of houses and castles, horses and dogs. I had no originality at all, contenting myself with making copies of pictures out of boys' annuals, or even out of the *Belfast Telegraph*, which came into our house two or three times a week. Father had a theory that there couldn't possibly be enough important news every day to fill the 'Tele', and that it was therefore a waste of money to buy it every day.

I remember the 'Tele' too because it was my first patron. Every Christmas it held a painting competition for boys and girls of various ages; and every year I put in my entry. I never succeeded in winning first, second or third prize but I never failed to win a consolation prize, and Christmas could never come round quickly enough for me to try to repeat my modest success. I continued to hope that one Christmas my name would appear among the real prize-winners in bold print, along with my address and the name of my school, but such fame evaded me, despite my strenuous efforts. Nevertheless all my relations were shown my name in small print and that was fame enough for me, at least for the time being.

The drawing classes in school offered no such inducements to my artistic ambition. Instead we spent hours and hours trying to draw perfect circles and ellipses which were later developed into cones and other forms. I became an expert in drawing pots – but nobody ever suggested that my pots might have flowers in them – and I became equally adept at drawing empty buckets. As far as I can recall there were no reproductions hanging on the walls to inspire us to further efforts, so I had left Mountpottinger long before I saw a real picture, and experienced the joy of a great painting.

The singing class was another half-hour of welcome relaxation. We were taught by the tonic sol-fa method, and we all loved to follow the teacher's hand as he closed his fist for doh and we dutifully, if not always tunefully, ascended and descended the scale, our eyes concentrating on that dictatorial gesturing hand. Our song book of airs and melodies had a Scottish and English bias, though there were a couple of lyrics by Tom Moore. Alas, I've forgotten most of the tunes except 'God Save The King' and that I don't often have occasion to sing. Still I enjoyed robust songs like 'Men of Harlech' and only wish I had that song book now to remind me of our repertoire. What I do remember is the sight of the little tuning fork that gave us the right note. I longed to handle it and hold it to my ear, but our teachers never allowed it out of their own hands. It was an object I longed to possess, and as a substitute I made music with a comb wrapped in tissue paper. Eventually I progressed to the jew's-harp.

The space in front of Mountpottinger was *called* the playground, but nobody ever played there for long, except in the morning for five or ten minutes, at lunch time, or after school: school was a place to get away from as soon as possible. Sometimes, for these short periods, we'd play races or tig or 'relievo' or 'bar-the-door' or 'churchy-one-over' until the principal appeared and the game would stop; or, in the afternoons, a teacher would order us home with a wave of the hand and a gruff, 'Clear off! Clear off!' The playground could be used for drill or physical jerks during proper school hours, but any other recreation wasn't encouraged. In the high wall separating the school from Musgrave's factory a small iron drinking fountain was an attraction not so much because of our thirst after a running game but more because a mouthful of water could be used for purposes other than quenching a thirst. At the apex of the playground, a narrow passageway led to the boys' lavatory where, if you opened your trouser buttons to relieve yourself, you were likely to be spat on from the front or grabbed from behind. So you used the lavatory only when you were sure of not being molested by the bigger boys. As for the row of small white bowls without privacy or paper, I never remember seeing them being used. I certainly never dared to use one; I would hang on painfully until school was over, and then I would rush home to the luxury of our outside lavatory.

Life at home in some ways resembled life at school. At school the teachers who threatened and used the cane were my enemies; at home I regarded father as my enemy, though he pretended to be my friend. When mother and I were alone in the kitchen I was happy; I was always glad when, after throwing my schoolbag in the hall, I discovered that father hadn't yet returned from work. Until he returned, the two of us could sit in peace, reading. Mother was a great reader of women's magazines such as *My Weekly* and the *Red Star*; and often when she collected them at the newsagent shop on the Albert Bridge Road she would also collect my *Rover* or *Adventure*. That was the kind of thing that made me love her: buying my magazines for me and leaving them on the table so that I could at once immerse myself in the stories and obliterate from my mind the horrors of school. She had the knack of anticipating my desires. To make my happiness complete she would often produce a bag of sweets for us to share while we settled down to our silent reading.

Then father would appear through the back door and our happiness would be broken.

'You're back early, Bob, aren't you?'

Father would look round the kitchen without replying. Mother would leave down her magazine on the sofa and go into the scullery to prepare his meal.

'Nothin' ready for me,' father would begin, taking off his dirty boots and throwing them against the fender.

'It'll be ready, Bob, when you're ready. You've to wash yourself, haven't you?'

'I'm hungry,' father would growl. 'Have ye potatoes on for me?'

'No. You'd potatoes yesterday, hadn't you?'

'You've nothin' hot then, have you?'

'No. But what do you want? I can run to the corner shop and get you whatever you want.'

With every word I would know that a row was inevitable, and that I would be somehow dragged into it; and I also recognised that mother was in the wrong for *not* having his meal ready. I would want to flee from the house and seek refuge in the street; but, afraid of what might happen to mother in my absence, I would stay on, pretending to read, but in fact waiting for the moment when father's surliness would flare into one of his uncontrollable tempers and he'd strike her, and I'd intervene with cries of rage and anguish, '*Don't father! Don't! Don't!*', attacking him with my own puny fists until he'd shout, 'Stop you! Git out a the way!'; and he'd take me by the arm and lead me into the hall, where I'd sit at the foot of the stairs sobbing.

After a row quietness would follow, and father would sit down to a makeshift meal of tea, bread and jam; or he might prepare potatoes for himself, disdaining any help from mother, and all the while casting up her faults. Often the kitchen door would open and father would give me a sad look, his face pale and drawn.

'The day'll come, son, when you'll understand.'

And I'd feel his hand touch my hair as he passed me on his way upstairs.

CHAPTER FOUR

Living at the lower end of our street I was more familiar with the
sordidness of Lord Street than with the respectability of Templemore Avenue. Rough families lived off Lord Street and the pubs
were always the centre of brawls; sometimes the police from
Mountpottinger barracks would appear on the scene, drawing
their batons to restore law and order. The only prosperous family
we knew in Lord Street owned the grocery shop opposite the Gut.
Mother was on very friendly terms with Mrs McDowell and ran
in and out of the shop three or four times a day. Father would
sneer at her for buying 'a quarter of this and a quarter of that',
wasting time on idle gossip, instead of giving the woman a decent
weekly order on a Friday. He alleged that mother was the greatest
gossip in our street and guilty of wasting not only her own time
but everybody else's. Certainly mother disliked housework and
hated being indoors with nobody to talk to all day, when she
could be in and out of neighbours' houses, or running unnecessary
messages to McDowell's or even taking a race to Carlton Street on
the Mountpottinger Road where granda and grandma Leeman lived.

Father continually warned me not to play near the Gut or in the
'wee field' but to stay in my own street and play games at the quiet
Templemore Avenue end. To him, the Avenue with its tall terrace
houses, each with a bow window, attic, bathroom, and indoor
lavatory, epitomized the height of respectability. To me, the
Avenue meant the public baths where I learnt to swim and dive,
the public library, where I borrowed books once or twice a week,
and the big cindery space near Madrid Street, where hobby-
horses, swings, and side-shows miraculously appeared at Easter
and Christmas and drew crowds from all over Ballymacarett.

One of father's ambitions was to move from Chatsworth Street
some day and rent a house in a quieter area. He'd no friends in the

street – mother had too many – and when he was on the late shift the noise made it impossible for him to get a decent rest. Besides, our two-bedroomed house became too small for us; our family increased and I'd a sister, six years younger than myself followed by my brother Jim, ten years younger. My sister had to be brought up in Carlton Street, and, as a result, I seldom saw her though she attended Mountpottinger. As for my baby brother, I'd little interest in him, regarding him as a competitor for mother's affection, and I could conceive of no reason why I should give him any share of my own affection.

We were, therefore, a divided family during the first decade of my life – divided in two senses. At home, father, mother and I made an unharmonious trio, but not always, of course. Sometimes all was well, father and mother would be on good terms, and they'd take us on trips to Bangor, Donaghadee or Newcastle on a free pass; or from time to time father would invite a railway man and his wife in for an evening's whist, a game father was fond of; after the whist – played in the parlour – we would go into the kitchen where the table would look splendid, covered with a fresh, white cloth and cups and saucers and plates of the same colour, instead of the usual odd bits and pieces. Mother would buy three or four different kinds of bread as well as an apple cake and maybe a lovely sponge cake with a layer of cream sandwiched in its middle. On these occasions, mother would look neat and glowing, her thick brown hair brushed off her forehead, a white brooch at her throat, and in a dress especially bought for the occasion. Then after supper, mother, whose temperament was too restless for cards, would volunteer to do the washing up and I would take her place at the table, and on her return father and the others would praise me for the hands I'd played. This was flattery because the truth was I'd too much of mother's temperament to be a good player. During these harmonious occasions father was always in the best of form, proud of mother's appearance, her high spirits and her ability to keep the chat lively between the games of whist.

The other family split was the classical one: father couldn't abide the sight of grandma and granda Leeman, and hadn't a good word to say about either of them. He never put a foot across their door if he could help it, though sometimes he just couldn't avoid a visit to Carlton Street, for instance whenever my younger sister was ill. When he did pay a visit it was with ill-concealed distaste, a duty which had to be undertaken, but which could be discharged in under ten minutes with hardly a word exchanged. Then with a curt, 'Cheerio, everybody', he'd take himself off to his own parents' house in Beechfield Street on the other side of the Mountpottinger Road; and there, according to mother, he'd sit for hours as if his behind were glued to the chair. Mother made fun of father's devotion to grandma Boyd whom he visited two or three times each week, and father complained constantly and bitterly of mother's attachment to grandma Leeman. 'Your mother spends twice as much time in Carlton Street than she does in her own home,' was his constant complaint.

As for myself, everybody seemed to be in tacit agreement that my role was that of go-between. At least once a week I'd pay a formal visit to the houses of both sets of grandparents. This I usually did on Sundays, taking care to spend the same length of time in each house. I set about visiting both sets of grandparents on Sunday mornings because Sunday was easily the longest day of the week. I mean, of course, the longest day of the week for me. There was nothing to do except go to church and Sunday school, and I wasn't enthusiastic about church-going, and the main reason I attended Sunday school was that I was ordered to do so, and it never entered my head to make a protest.

Carlton Street was a short cul-de-sac of kitchen houses, with grandma Leeman's house having an advantage over the others: an old-fashioned street lamp on the outside wall threw light into the kitchen in the evening so that they seldom had to put a penny into the gas meter; and as they cooked on the kitchen fire, they were able to live very economically. But they were so mean – according to father – that you'd never see a flame in the grate in a month of Sundays, a saying that took me a long time to make sense of, because it sounded so nonsensical. It wasn't true either, because I'd seen a big blazing fire one weekday when I called in after school and grandma was baking soda and potato farls on the griddle. This was the time I got into trouble.

Grandma was alone and as it was a cold afternoon she let me sit up close to the fire and watch her at her work. She was never at any time a great one for chatting to me, and when she was baking she scarcely paid me any attention at all. I might as well not have been there, for she never threw a glance in my direction. However, I didn't in the least mind being ignored because I loved the sight of the griddle and the smell of the farls and the heat of the fire. I was looking forward to the time when grandma would feather a soda farl off the griddle, let it cool, but not for too long because I liked it still warm with plenty of melted butter. . . Perhaps I was anticipating my treat, when I happened to put my hand close to the griddle and something struck me on the back of my hand. A blob of blood appeared.

'You shouldn't do that!' grandma shouted, holding the bread knife in her hand.

'I was doing nothing!'

'You were touchin' the bread!'

'No I wasn't!' I protested, bursting into tears. 'I wasn't! I wasn't!'

Overcome with shock and fear at the injustice, I wouldn't let her touch my hand but protected it with my other hand; I'd have rushed out of the kitchen only that I couldn't go home without my schoolbag and with my hand all blood.

'I didn't mean to hurt you, child dear. Only meant to scare you. Come and give me a kiss.'

But I shook my head, still weeping, and grandma led me into the scullery and put my hand under the water tap. Then she went upstairs and came back with a piece of white cloth that looked like the tail of an old shirt. She skilfully made a bandage, wrapped it round my hand and tried to comfort me.

At home, when I explained what had happened, mother made light of my injury – a deep cut of about an inch – but father was furious and began to shout.

'Was the oul' lady drunk? That's what I'd like to know.'

'It was a mistake I told you,' mother retorted. 'Anybody can make a mistake, can't they? Anybody but you!'

'D'you expect me to believe any sober bein' would wound a child wi' a knife?' Then to me: 'Listen here, you're not to go next nor near Carlton Street till I let you! Mind what I tell you.' For a long time, maybe six months, I didn't go back; but finally the incident was forgiven if not forgotten, for father remembered it all of his life. And so have I. I once heard – I suppose it must have been father who told me – that grandma Leeman had a vicious temper; if so, this was the only occasion I saw her display it.

Other than this incident I remember little about her; but recently, I came across an old family album, and discovered a faded photograph of her as a young woman. To my astonishment I found her exceptionally beautiful – she had a perfect figure and finely chiselled features. But as I recall her in her middle age, she'd lost her looks and figure and had turned into a snuff-taking old woman with a pasty complexion, no pride in her appearance and with a permanent air of discontent.

Granda Leeman, who spent most of his leisure sitting in front of the fire, whether lit or out, smoking his pipe, whether lit or out, and spitting into a spittoon at his side – and sometimes missing it – looked ferocious until he stood up and moved. Then his ferociousness disappeared and you saw a small barrel of a man with dim, almost vacant, light blue eyes and a gruff voice. He had to be coaxed to talk, but as soon as he got properly going he hated to be interrupted. Unfortunately he was so longwinded that I couldn't listen to him for more than five minutes without my attention wandering, particularly when he decided to inform me about the prospects of the world's shipbuilding industry. But when he talked about his voyages in ships undergoing trials I listened to every word he uttered, though I didn't believe all of his tales. He told me he'd travelled round the Mediterranean more than once, yet I found it strange he couldn't recall the name of a single port where his ship had called. If I tried to elicit geographical information he'd cut me off with a wave of his hand or a probing of his pipe and 'Ach, how cud an oul' fella like me mind them kind a things. I was kept that busy anyway, paintin' the state-rooms an' the cabins. Sometimes, I tell ye, I hardly seen daylight for a week.

35

Didn't know the time o' the day it was. . . Or what day of the week either. . . Or where on earth we were. Or where we were goin'. . . Or where we'd been. . . A painter on a ship hasn't the time t'bother wi' all them kind a things. . . He's far too busy wi' his brushes. . . Too busy gittin' ready for his work. An' too busy gittin' redd up when he's it done.' But one time when he was going full steam ahead grandma blasted him, 'Ach Jimmy, stop fillin' up that child's head wi blethers! Sure you've niver been no place 'cept to the north coast o' Scotland or thereabouts!'

After that outburst granda Leeman preferred to tell me about the great games of football he'd seen when he was working in Birkenhead in England and went every Saturday to support Liverpool or Everton. He knew that I was mad keen on football and that I attended the Oval – Glentoran's ground – to see the matches. I always arrived early – at least half an hour before the kick off – and would stand just outside the turnstiles.

'Give me a lift over, mister?'

If I was lucky somebody would invite me into the queue and help me to vault over the turnstile, then I'd run up the terrace slope to find a place at the railings so that I could have a close view of the game. Neither father nor mother knew about this – it was a kind of begging, and I was a bit ashamed of myself for doing it. But I didn't think it wrong, for other boys went with their fathers and got lifted over the turnstiles free. It was my bad luck not to have a father who supported Glentoran and frequented the Oval every other Saturday. I would have loved granda Leeman to take me with him, seeing that he was once fond of football, and I gave him more than a hint or two, but all to no avail. Either he was too stupid to take a hint, or else he'd lost all interest in football and couldn't be bothered to take it up again, even with the advantage of having my company. But I'd a suspicion he didn't really like me, and I can remember grandma saying to him once when I was sitting on the stairs reading, but with my ears open: 'Oh, he's a Boyd all right, he takes after *them*!' I knew what that meant, but didn't see any reason why I should take after either side – the Boyds or the Leemans. All I wanted was to be myself.

On Sunday mornings, after my half hour in Carlton Street, I proceeded to Beechfield Street to pay my respects to father's parents. Theirs was a parlour house with a bow window and a tiny garden at the front; and inside it was comfortably furnished. I was always made welcome at once. 'Ah, look who's arrived!' or 'We've got a visitor!' or 'Come in and tell us your news!' I'd be speeded along the hall and ordered to sit down; then questions would be fired at me, so fast I would hardly have time to answer them, mostly about school – what I was studying, what subjects I liked best, what I wanted to be when I grew up. Here, in contrast to Carlton Street, I became the centre of interest, and my visit would be rounded off not only with a glass of milk and a bun, but also with something to put in my trousers pocket – a couple of pennies – and a warning which I didn't know whether to take seriously or not: 'Mind an' don't spend both in the same shop!' Usually I didn't, on the principle that a visit to two shops was twice as pleasurable as a visit to one.

Granda Boyd resembled my father in appearance; he was tall and rather stern looking, and when he laughed he gave a guffaw exactly like father's. He also walked like father – splay-footed, and stood the same way, as if rooted to the ground. This posture and walk weren't characteristic of the Boyd males, but were peculiar to granda Boyd and father, both engine-drivers. An engine-driver stands for hours on the footplate every day, and in order to balance himself he keeps his feet apart, so engine-drivers tend to be splay-footed. At least that was the explanation I got when I asked why father and granda Boyd stood and walked the same way. As usual all the family entered into a discussion on the matter, and the conclusion satisfied me.

Grandma Boyd, a well set-up woman with a matriarchal presence, was the most taciturn of the family, but her word carried the most weight. She gave the impression of being fond of people, especially her own grown-up family, but of them all – I'd three uncles and three aunts – she was supposed to favour father. This I don't believe to be true – aunt Ethel or aunt Alice was my informant – but if it was true it was only because father visited her so regularly and confided in her so closely. Mother resented father's devotion to grandma Boyd; I once heard her say: 'Your father's fonder of her than he is of me.' If that was true, then no wonder mother resented her; but I'm not sure it had always been so, or was so.

I liked all of my father's brothers and sisters, though I had my favourites. Uncle Willie, at this time my only married uncle, didn't visit Beechfield Street as often as father did, probably because his own home off the Ormeau Road was too far away from Bally-macarett, and aunt Ida wasn't a great one for visiting relations – either her own family or the family she married into. She had the reputation of doing what she pleased and of persuading Uncle Willie to do likewise. But she encouraged me to visit their house on the Ormeau Road; and I liked visiting them because the journey involved a walk through the Ormeau Park, a trip across the Lagan on a rowing boat, and finally a reward of sixpence or even a shilling for taking the trouble of going out of my way to see them both. They had no children of their own and fussed over me so much that I always felt important in their company.

Because I was fond of reading, the opinion of the family in Beechfield Street was that I would 'take after' uncle Willie, the oldest of my uncles and a collector of books, particularly books on economics, politics and trade-unionism; books, according to my aunts, so dry and deep that even Willie found them hard to tackle; and if he found them hard what hope had ignoramuses like themselves of understanding them? Uncle Willie had always been interested in such subjects even when he was an apprentice to his trade of carpentry; and he wasn't long out of his time before he became a full-time secretary of the National Union of Vehicle Builders. Granda Boyd himself had been a pioneer trade-unionist in the railway, and uncle Tommy, father's younger brother, was every bit as keen on union activities as uncle Willie, though he was far too retiring by nature to push himself forward for office. He too was a carpenter by trade. As for my youngest uncle – Herbie – he was handicapped by bad eyesight and had never been accepted for a trade. Instead he was given odd jobs as a labourer, mostly in the Sirocco Works, where he was friendly with a foreman who took an interest in his welfare.

Of my aunts, my favourite was aunt Ethel, who had the reputation of being the liveliest and most talkative of the three, though
aunt Alice, who never married, had the sharpest tongue. Aunt
Lizzie, the eldest, was already married when I was attending
Mountpottinger school and her husband, Joe Moreland, had the
sourest expression of any man I ever knew. An electrician by
trade, he too was an advocate of trade-unionism but considered
that any meddling with politics was a waste of time, all politicians
being rogues out to fill their own pockets and empty other
people's.

So the two families I favoured with my weekly visits had little in
common and as the go-between I had to tread carefully between
them. In particular I had to be careful about what I said; because
grown-ups, I soon discovered, seemed quite incapable of res-
pecting what I intended as confidential information. My remarks
might just as well have been printed in the *Belfast Telegraph* so
quickly did they circulate. Naturally I got into trouble for
blabbing out things I'd overheard and wasn't supposed to know.
My problem was that of any go-between: not knowing what to
keep to myself.
    Uncle Willie and uncle Tommy were socialists, and therefore
automatically voted Labour at elections, but I could never, no
matter how hard I tried, share their enthusiasm for politics. I
seemed to be taking after my father, who voted Labour only
because his brothers did, not from any conviction of his own.
Socialism didn't appear to have anything special to offer me. It
was supposed to have a flag – the Red Flag – but I'd never seen it
hung from a window in our street, or from a window in a Catholic
street, such as Seaforde Street, opposite Beechfield Street. Apparently Catholics had no more love for the Red Flag than Protestants. Indeed they had strange flags of their own: the Tricolour,
which was the flag of Ireland; and the papal flag, which was in
honour of the Pope of Rome. They hated the British and they
hated us Protestants, and above all, they hated the Union Jack. I
couldn't understand why. Nor could I understand why granda
Leeman called himself an Orangeman, parading on the Twelfth of

July behind a flute band all the way to a field to listen to speeches by politicians and clergymen, when he'd no interest at all in politics or in anything else except decorating ships and drinking porter and spitting into his spittoon!

Everything seemed mixed up to me; I didn't know what to think about politics and flags. All I knew was that I liked to listen to a band: a flute band on parade in Ballymacarett; a Salvation Army band playing in the Citadel in Carlton Street; a brass band playing in the Ormeau or Victoria Park. I'd never heard or seen a Catholic band. The only Catholics I'd ever seen were in Seaforde Street but I never dared go near them. That would have been asking for trouble.

Then something curious happened: my Boyd grandparents left Beechfield Street, swopping their house with a Catholic family who lived in Portallo Street up the Castlereagh Road. Now that was an extraordinary thing and I certainly couldn't comprehend it, not at first anyway. But once it had been explained to me it became quite clear. It was the time of what we called 'the riots'. We didn't know where or when or why they broke out, except that it wasn't our fault but the fault of the Catholics. Everybody said that, at least everybody I spoke to in our street: the Catholics always started the riots and were to blame for everything that happened afterwards. But why were they so evil? That puzzled me and I thought it must have something to do with the Pope in Rome.

Anyway, I was told that the Boyds had heard of a Catholic family who were scared of being chased out of their house which was in a Protestant area, and they wanted to get out before this happened. When granda and grandma heard of this they met the Catholics and agreed to switch houses because Beechfield Street was adjoining the small Catholic area of Ballymacarett. They would be doing the Catholic family a good turn and doing themselves a good turn too. As well as that, the air up the Castlereagh Road was much fresher than the air down the Mountpottinger Road, which had a bone-yard, and the stench of it would make you vomit if you didn't hold your breath and put your hand over your mouth and nose.

As Carlton Street was on the Mountpottinger Road I thought

that maybe granda and grandma Leeman might want to do a swop too. But no, they wouldn't do such a thing; Carlton Street was a good Protestant street, not like Beechfield Street which was mixed, and getting more Catholic very year.

All this changed my Sunday visiting. Before the swop I could visit both the Leemans and the Boyds on the same morning: now I had to choose which way to go each Sunday. I had to keep the balance right, else I'd be in trouble. The upshot was that I lay in bed longer and didn't bother to go anywhere except into the street to look for company. Or else I went all the way to Hatfield Street in the Ormeau Road where uncle Willie and aunt Ida lived.

No wonder then that I lacked enthusiasm for politics. Politics seemed to upset everybody so that you didn't know what to think. It was all very confusing. The only sensible people appeared to be my three aunts – aunt Lizzie, aunt Ethel and aunt Alice. They were all in agreement that there should be no talk about politics in the house, and that a youngster shouldn't have to listen to such nonsense. Plenty of time later on if I was that way inclined. But they all hoped I wouldn't be; that I'd have more sense. 'But aunt Ida says –' I once began to protest. They guessed what I was going to say, and aunt Alice shut me up.

'Never you mind what your aunt Ida says. Besides, she isn't your real aunt. Politics is all she has to think of. She'd be better off looking after her house and our Willie's health.'

It seemed to me that aunt Ida looked after her house and her husband very well indeed.

41

I was able to endure school only because I lived mostly in my imagination. Even when I was engaged in learning spellings or rhyming over Latin roots, my imagination would take me far from the buzz of the classroom. It was impossible for me to concentrate on lessons all day, and impossible for all of us to sit still with our arms folded and our backs straight, and not open our mouths unless in answer to a question. The threat of the cane, or the sight of it produced from behind the blackboard, or the sudden yelp of pain as someone was punished would transport me back to the real world. And the real world of the classroom could only be endured if I was able to escape from it by way of my imagination.

In school I often turned my thoughts to the pigeons in the blue loft two backyards away from our backyard. I loved to watch them appear in the sky, settle on the roof tops and swoop to the white ledge in front of their loft before disappearing inside. They were racing pigeons and were supposed to fly all the way home from somewhere in England, or even from France. But that I found hard to believe. There were also 'strays' to be found in our street, nibbling between the pavers in search of food. I pitied them because they'd no loft to shelter in at night and no one to leave corn for them when they were hungry. There were sparrows too, but I hadn't much interest in them. Robins were different; they seldom came down to the pavers, but when they did I tried to get as close as I could, to see how red their breasts were.

The sense of form and rhythm and colour I should have learnt in school I learnt in the street. For instance, I loved kites: not only flying them – though it was wonderful on a windy day to follow my kite spiralling towards the fleecy clouds above the chimneys – but also going to Anderson's shop to select my kite for its colour, taking it home cradled in my arms, inspecting it all the while for its ability to fly and to survive crashes. Bought kites were flimsy affairs; home-made ones were more durable and better flyers. It was a good plan to take a homemade kite to the open space we called the Dyke, a shortened form for Klondyke, where you could run for more than a hundred yards to get your kite air-borne and there was no danger of getting it entangled round a chimneypot and lost.

The Dyke was the only sizable open space near our street, and was a place I loved, though I suppose it must have been a bit of a dump; it was treeless and flowerless, except for the odd dandelion and daisy, and at one end, bounded by a rusty corrugated iron paling, the ground was pitted with large holes, some dry and some full of stagnant water, but these were a challenge to a cowboy galloping away from bloodthirsty red Indians. The holes became secret caverns; the mounds of cindery earth, mountains; the pools of scummy water, lakes; and the whole dump, a territory in the Wild West. And the Dyke had something else to offer. There were layers of damp clay in some of the holes, and all sorts of figures could be shaped out of the clay with the help of two bits of slate or wood which you were bound to come across if you searched the Dyke.

Although we boys were far too proud to be seen playing with the girls in our street – for to be seen meant being called 'wee jenny' and jeered at – I liked watching the girls at their games, especially skipping. If none of my companions were about and the girls were skipping near me, the temptation would be too great and I'd join in. At first they might make a protest, but eventually some girl – more tolerant than the rest – would accept my participation, saying, 'Let the wee fella play!' but adding the proviso 'As long as he takes an end.' When my turn came to take an end of the skipping rope, I would keep a good look-out for the sudden appearance of other boys, and if any appeared I'd hastily throw the rope away and pretend I wasn't playing. What *was* permitted by our code of masculine behaviour was to borrow a skipping rope from the girls in order to give a solo performance, and by 'showing off' prove that a boy could skip faster than any girl. But

43

this contention could be easily disproved, and was, because girls got more practice than any boy, and would immediately take up the challenge to display their superior skill.

What I couldn't understand about girls was their silly habit of playing with dolls. One of them would borrow a mat from her hall, sit on it and play with her doll, dressing and undressing it and changing its clothes and even washing its face. Then another girl would appear with another doll, and the new doll would be given the same treatment. Before long, more mats would be borrowed from the hall, and maybe a chair or a stool from inside and gradually something called a 'house' would be created – most of it in their imagination but with enough bits and pieces collected from their homes to give their creation an air of verisimilitude. Usually unable to find or borrow broken cups, plates and saucers, they had to be content with what they called 'babby dishes': odds and ends, including bits of coloured glass, gathered up from the street, the 'wee field' and the smelly back-entries.

Girls also loved dressing up, and singing and dancing. When spring came, the May Queen appeared and all the girls combined to beg, borrow or steal scraps of cast-off clothing: scarves, veils and any odd bits of silk or satin that could be rummaged from drawer or cupboard, and washed to be made presentable for display in the street. The girls would parade themselves in a wealth of colour, the May Queen in front with head raised high, her followers shouting in lusty unison:

The darkie said he'd marry her,
Marry her, marry her,
The darkie said he'd marry her
Because she was the Queen. . .

And when the May Queen appeared in all her glory, the girls would take over the street, marching up and down, the neighbours out at the front doors nodding their heads and laughing and clapping their hands. As for us, we skulked along the shady side of the street, mimicking the singing and dancing and pretending that we were enjoying ourselves too. But the sun shone on the happy faces of the girls and nobody paid any attention to us.

There were occasions, however, when the inviolable law separating us from the girls would be forgotten and we'd joyfully participate in a game like 'Here are the robbers'. It was a good game. I liked the song and the mysterious story with its crisis of a rough tug-o-war which allowed us to put our arms round the girls' waists. Then somebody would say, 'Again', and the song and its story of robbers being imprisoned and offered 'oranges or lemons' would begin again:

Here are the robbers coming through,
Coming through, coming through,
Here are the robbers coming through,
My fair lady.
What did the robbers do on you,
Do on you, do on you?
What did the robbers do on you,
My fair lady?
They broke my watch and they stole my chain,
Stole my chain, stole my chain,
They broke my watch and they stole my chain,
My fair lady. . .

After a while the story would lose its mystery and its freshness, the ritual would become stale, and we'd tire of the tug-o-war. The girls would drift away as they were called indoors and we would end the day with a rough game like 'churchy-one-over' which no girl dared play because if she did she'd show her knickers. That was something the girls in our street hated to do.

But there was one exception: a girl called Lily Morris who lived with her mother in the house facing the lamp-post in the middle of the street. Lily was a big girl with bouncy breasts who liked to play with us if we'd let her, and sometimes we did. People whispered that Lily looked like taking after her mother who worked in a warehouse somewhere in town, and who left Lily to mind the house every day after school. She was the only girl in the whole of our street who'd show her knickers if no grown ups were about. She wouldn't always show them – sometimes she'd hit you if you tried to touch her – but at other times she didn't object. Once she followed us to the Dyke and three of us caught hold of her and took her knickers down to find what she was hiding underneath. It wasn't much, you could see hardly anything at all, yet she screamed when we all took turns to touch it, and said she'd tell on us. But she never did. I heard she went to the Dyke with other boys from Paxton Street. I heard, too, that her mother let men in by the back door after dark on winter nights. But I never saw anybody go into the Morris house, back door or front door. People said that Lily had a father somewhere but he never came to the house. Others said she had no father at all. But I knew that couldn't be true. Everybody had to have a father, else they couldn't be born. We had talked in the Dyke about what a father had to do to become a father, but it seemed so funny that we all laughed at it. Then one day Tom Prichard told us that he'd seen his father lying on top of his mother in the front bedroom. They'd left the bedroom door slightly open, and he had peeped in. He told us too that they were wrestling all the time and laughing as well. He just peeped in – that was all – then he tiptoed downstairs and ran out of the house. We all believed him because he wet his finger and crossed his throat. But all the same I found it hard to convince myself he was telling the truth. Didn't everybody tell lies at times? It was supposed to be wrong, and in our Sunday school we were warned never to tell lies; but I suspected that everybody did. To keep out of trouble we cheated and lied every day, and I don't think any of us suffered much from a bad conscience. I know I didn't.

During my six years at Mountpottinger I never once achieved my aim of becoming top boy for the week. There were about fifty of us and I usually was placed in the first ten. Sometimes I reached the first five, and once I was second, but never first. Every Friday afternoon our marks for the week were totted up and on Monday mornings the new order in the class was announced, and you were moved up or down according to your new marks. As long as I was placed in the first ten I was quite pleased, but occasionally my marks were so poor that I found myself down in the lower half of

46

the class, and Mr Watson, our sixth-class teacher, would give me a sour look and say, 'What are you doing down among the duffers?' My response would be to drop my head in acknowledgement of my humiliation. 'You're supposed to be scholarship material,' he'd say. I never supposed myself to be any kind of material and knew nothing about scholarships except that as a result of doing well in an examination your education would continue in another school; and this didn't seem at all an attractive prospect to me. The sooner I was finished with school the better I'd be pleased.

However this prospect began to be discussed every time I visited Portallo Street or Hatfield Street. I was asked what I wanted to be when I grew up, and as I hadn't the slightest notion I always said, 'I don't know.' Then an interrogation would follow: 'Would you like to be an engine-driver? Or a clerk? Or a clergyman?' These seemed to me stupid questions to which I couldn't give satisfactory answers. Yet it appeared my future was so important that the whole of the Boyd family had involved themselves in it. The Leemans were considered to be useless in such matters.

When I asked my class mates what they intended to do when *they* left school, they were just as vague as myself. My best friend, a delicate boy called Skelton, admitted that he wanted to become a fireman, like his father. Of all the suggestions that had been put to me that seemed by far the most attractive: wearing a uniform and a brass helmet; riding on a fire-engine through the town; climbing long ladders to rescue people; directing a hose to jet water high into a burning building until the flames were extinguished – what could be more exciting? But I kept this notion to myself, as I did the notion of going to sea as a midshipman and sailing round the world; or of being an intrepid explorer in Africa and trudging through swamps and jungles and over mountains where no white man's foot had ever trod. I'd plenty of ideas, but enough sense to know that none of them would be acceptable.

I also fancied what every boy is supposed to fancy: being an engine-driver; but father had a strong prejudice against my having anything to do with a steam locomotive – indeed having anything to do with the railway at all. The assumption of the family was that I was destined for better things. It would be a great mistake if

I ever took off my coat and dirtied my hands: I must at all costs avoid manual work and try to find a good clean job with a pension. I should try to emulate my uncle Willie, the only member of the family who'd succeeded in throwing off his overalls and now enjoyed the prestige of going to an office in decent clothes. Father told me often that one of the many disadvantages of being an engine-driver was that when you finished work you'd to spend extra time changing out of your dirty dungarees, washing, getting into clean clothes, and by the time you'd done that and had your meal all you felt fit for was a lie-down on the sofa and a sleep, and then the whole evening was gone, wasted. Father believed that cleanliness was next to godliness, and consequently this daily ritual after work took him nearly an hour. The worst part of it was his shaving. Father used an old cut-throat razor which he kept in a black case out of everybody's reach but his own. No matter how thoroughly he stropped it and soaped his face he nearly always cut his chin or cheek. 'God, I've cut myself again,' he'd shout from the scullery.

'How did that happen?' mother would ask him.

'The bad light in this oul' scullery!'

Our house was gaslit, but there was no mantle in the scullery so father had to shave by candlelight.

Like father, I washed myself in the scullery in the mornings; to my own satisfaction, if to nobody else's. For before I could reach the front door on my way out to school mother would always give me a shout.

'Here, let me see your neck! Did you wash it this morning?'

'Yes I did, mother!' I'd protest, imagining that I had.

'Let me see.'

The top of my woollen jersey would be turned down and my neck carefully scrutinised, then the verdict was given.

'You mustn't have touched this neck of yours for a fortnight!'

I would assure her to the contrary.

'How is it then that there's a black ring round it – as black as your boots?'

Mother would lead me back to the scullery, lift the rough facecloth that was always lying on top of a bar of Lifebuoy soap, and scrub my neck until it hurt and I'd cry, 'That's enough. I'll be late for school!'

So I could sympathise with father when he complained about the grime he had to get rid of at the end of his day's work; I seemed to get grimy after only playing in the street. I hated washing just as much as father hated shaving. In my opinion, if I washed myself at night before going to bed there was no need to wash again in the morning. After all, you couldn't get dirty lying in bed, so I'd content myself with what mother called 'a cat's lick'. Anyway washing yourself in our scullery was always a problem and father would take himself off once a week to the Templemore baths for a proper bath. Occasionally I was given the money to go as well, but instead I would opt for the big swimming bath; I'd soap myself all over in the shower first, and then I'd enjoy a long swim. But of course I said nothing about this. As long as I looked clean when I returned home, my hair still wet, all was well and no questions were asked.

Because Willie Skelton lived in the fire brigade station on the Albert Bridge Road we walked home from school together for part of the way. Sometimes I accompanied him as far as the fire station itself not only for the pleasure of his company but for the pleasure of being allowed to see the shining fire-engines with their beautifully polished brasswork standing at the ready, their bonnets pointing towards the wide doors so that if a call came in the crew would be in their places and off to the fire within minutes. I could imagine no other job that could give me so much pleasure, and if Willie – who had legs like match sticks and was hen-toed as well – could become a fireman, then my own chances were certainly better than his – unless of course he had the advantage of the mysterious and all-powerful 'influence', which father introduced into every discussion about my future prospects in life; he claimed to have a little influence in the railway, but doubted whether he'd enough to get me started as a clerk. Anyway clerking had no appeal to me whatsoever. Sitting at a desk in an office all day long struck me as no better than sitting at a desk in school, and already I'd had too much experience of that.

I was friendly with Willie for about a year when an accident occurred that ended our friendship. One day I invited him to play cricket with me in the 'wee field'. Having chalked up wickets on the Constance Street wall I made a practice drive with my home-made bat, and hit poor Willie bang on the forehead. He dropped to the ground stunned, and blood began to flow from his wound. Crying with pain and fright he ran home at once, leaving his schoolbag behind. I was so frightened myself that I didn't know what to do, and hadn't the courage to run after him with his bag, so I brought it home and left it in our hall alongside my own. The next morning when Willie didn't appear at school I imagined that I had killed him. If I had, then I'd be a murderer, and if I'd committed a murder what would happen to me? Would I be put in prison and hanged?

Willie was kept away from school for a whole week, and I convinced myself that he was dead. I prayed that he hadn't told on me but feared that somehow I would be found out, which I knew I would be – because in all the stories I had ever read evil deeds were always punished. All that long week I suffered from fear and remorse. Then on the following Monday Willie arrived at our house with a bandage round his head and lifted his bag. All he said was that he wasn't allowed to play with me any more. And that was the end of our friendship. In a way I was relieved because I was frightened of what his father and mother might say to me if ever I went near the fire station. For although what I'd done had been an accident – I wouldn't have hurt Willie for the world – his parents must have thought I'd done it on purpose. Yet Willie himself must have known that I would never have harmed him. Did he explain to them exactly what had happened? I never had the chance of asking him, for when I looked in his direction he would always turn his face away. Anyway I don't think I'd have been able to express my sorrow for what I'd done; but if we had become friends again I'd have given him something I valued – maybe part of my meccano set or a set of my cigarette-cards and then there would have been no need for me to say anything at all. My guilt lingered on, and mother noticed that Willie never called for me, but I never told her why.

At last I reached the sixth class, the class which was regarded as the most important one in the school because at the end of it a dozen or so of us would be selected as candidates for the city scholarships. Throughout the year our teachers impressed upon us that if we didn't work hard we wouldn't be permitted to enter for the examination. Every lesson had to be thoroughly learnt, every exercise at home perfectly done, and no bad behaviour in class would be tolerated. There would also be extra classes from three o'clock to half-past three for scholarship entrants.

Our two teachers were Mr McKee and Mr Watson, and we often noticed them consulting each other about the progress of each potential scholarship winner. As my parents had agreed to allow me to enter for the exam, my place in the class was noted every week. Then one day shortly after Christmas Mr McKee called me up to his high desk in the big room and told me that the final selection had been made.

'If you continue to work hard I've no doubt you'll succeed. You certainly have the ability.'

To my surprise he patted me on the head and smiled. I'd never noticed him smile before, and he'd never touched me before except to ask me to hold out my hand. Because of his baldness we naturally nicknamed him 'Old Baldy' but always in a whispered aside, as if even to whisper the nickname might get us into unimaginable trouble. We stood in absolute terror of him, watchful of every step he took and every look he gave. He was unquestionably a most conscientious headmaster and wholeheartedly gave his energy to turning us all from an unruly gang of street kids into a class as disciplined as young soldiers. My conviction now is that he was a kindly man whose defect was over-conscientiousness: he took his duties much too seriously. Mr McKee dressed well, better than any other grown-up I knew with the exception of Dr Williamson, and always wore a white shirt with a butterfly collar. When he was angry his face would change colour and his right hand, in which the cane was tightly grasped, would tremble, and he'd give the desk a resounding blow which would scatter the pile of exercise books onto the floor. We'd all stare wide-eyed, wondering what would happen next. If thunder

51

had rumbled in the sky and lightning lit up the big room none of us would have been in the least surprised.

Mr Watson, the senior teacher, was nicknamed 'Piggy' because of his broken nose. He was supposed to have been a boxer before he'd become a teacher. He was just as formidable as Mr McKee, and we were equally terrified of both. His gruff voice commanded immediate silence in the class, and when he stalked round the classroom, cane in hand, I used to pray that his attention wouldn't land on my jotter. What surprised us, from time to time, was his habit of breaking out into bursts of gurgling laughter which seemed to be uncontrollable; we would burst into laughter too, until we also lost control and had to be brought to heel with a bark: *'Quiet!'* That word was sufficient to snuff it out at once and silence would be restored.

We Mountpottinger boys were a pretty mixed bunch; we were drawn mostly from the neighbourhood and from working-class homes; but we tended to come from slightly better-off families, our fathers being tradesmen or indeed small shopkeepers. In my class there was one boy who lived somewhere in the country beyond the Cregagh tram-lines. He lived on a farm, had rosy cheeks and told us that he drank a pint of milk every day. Another boy lived in the suburbs at Knock and told us that his father was captain of a ship that sailed all over the world. And there was another poorly dressed boy called Gordon who was always wiping his dirty nose with the sleeve of his jersey and sniffling when everybody else was silent. He lived on the Newtownards Road, always came to school alone, never joined in the games of 'tig' in the playground, sat by himself in the classrooms, and his neighbours edged away as far as they could from him. And he made his way home alone. Sturdily built, he was never in any danger of being bullied; but Gordon was subjected to a worse punishment than any form of bullying: ostracism. No boy spoke to him and the teachers ignored him, yet he seldom missed a day though he led the life of an outcast. He smelt of stale fish so strongly that the boys sitting near him would put their fingers to their noses when the teachers were out of the classroom for a few minutes. Gordon had the saddest face I ever saw on any boy and I

52

should like to have befriended him but lacked the courage to approach him. I pitied him, but my pity didn't extend as far as speaking to him.

One morning, when Baldy was called out of our classroom on some business and we were all sitting quietly preparing our Latin roots, the boys next to Gordon began edging away from him, their hands to their noses. Then a boy from behind edged up close to him with a match-box in his hand.

'What are you doin'?' someone asked.

'Tryin' to catch one,' came the answer, and we all burst out into laughter.

At this moment Baldy reappeared.

'What's going on here?' he asked.

Nobody spoke.

'I've asked a question. What's going on here?'

No answer.

'Gordon, is it you?'

Gordon shook his head and stared into space.

'Are you sure?'

Gordon stared into space.

'Perfectly sure?'

Tears welled up in his eyes and trickled down his cheeks. But he said nothing. The boys who'd edged away from him slowly edged back to their original seats. Then Baldy noticed the match-box.

'What's that you have, boy, in your hand?'

'A match-box, sir.'

'Were you lighting matches, boy?'

'Oh no, sir.'

'Hand over that match-box.'

He handed it over and it was seen to be empty.

'Is this some silly trick you were playing in my absence?'

'No, sir.'

'Then what were you doing with this box?'

'It was Gordon, sir.'

'Oh, so it was Gordon. What was Gordon doing?'

'There's fleas on his back, sir.'

'Oh, is that so?'

'Yes, sir. I caught one, sir. But it got away, sir. It jumped. They all jump, sir. You can't catch them, sir.'

Baldy said nothing more. We went on memorising our Latin roots from the tattered little booklet. We would hide it on our thighs when we were given the command, 'All books down', and leave it open so that we could lower our eyes and peep at the roots without the teacher noticing anything. If he came close you could surreptitiously push the booklet further up your thigh, well out of sight. Then you'd take care not to move, else the root-book might fall to the floor and you'd be found out. Then you were for the cane, maybe one on each hand.

At the end of the half-hour in the classroom Baldy marched us into the big room where we had to go round the ring for sums. Gordon was marching with the rest of us when Baldy shouted, 'Gordon!' That was all. Gordon was sent home that day and never returned. I heard he was sent to Westbourne School on the Newtownards Road, but the only time I ever saw him again was when I went into a fish and chip shop after I'd been to a matinee to the New Princess. He was wearing an apron and didn't let on he knew me when I asked for my pennyworth of chips. He wrapped them up in a piece of newspaper and handed them to me without a word. He looked as sad as ever.

I never went back there again, though I thought of him often enough.

In the early spring of 1924 – when I was eleven and a half and my future education was being debated in Portallo Street, sometimes in my presence, and sometimes in my absence – I fell ill and Dr Williamson informed my father and mother that I'd have to be sent to Purdysburn fever hospital. I had scarlatina, and he arranged for the ambulance to come for me at once. When it arrived I was carried out in father's strong arms and a small crowd gathered to see my departure. Before the door closed I noticed that mother and father were crying. Then the door shut and I was lying on a bed covered with warm blankets.

On my arrival at the hospital the nurse told me that I'd have to take a bath.

'Can you bath yourself? Do you feel strong enough?'

I nodded.

'You're just too old for me to bath you,' she said smiling, as if to say, 'You'd have liked that, wouldn't you?'

For weeks I lay in bed with nothing to do all day – no books or magazines were permitted because of the risk of infection. I thought the time would never come when I'd be allowed to get up and walk about the ward, helping the nurses to make the beds and carrying the bottles for peeing into to and from the other patients. But at last I was told I was getting well and would be allowed out of bed.

I enjoyed my convalescence. A friendly nurse on night duty let me sit on a chair beside her, and even let me sit on her knee for a while before saying, 'Now, that's enough. . . You'll be able to go asleep now, won't you?' She'd put me to bed, and after giving me a peck of a kiss and smoothing the bedclothes she'd add, 'Now be a good boy and go asleep', which was easier said than done.

The morning came when I was to go home. It was strange to be back in our small kitchen, and stranger still to be lying in my own bed with the walls so close, and the shouts coming up from the corner-boys in Lord Street. I wasn't allowed to return to school for another fortnight, and I'd now missed so many days at school that I wasn't sure whether I'd be permitted to enter the scholar-ship exam at the end of May. I *was* sure, however, that I no longer wanted to enter for it. But I'd no choice in the matter; the decision was made for me. On my first day back at school Mr McKee said he was glad to see me looking so well and added that I'd have to work extra hard now, but he was confident that I'd do my best for the honour of the school. I rejoined the dozen boys selected for extra homework and extra classes and envied the remainder of the class who were allowed to work at a more leisurely pace.

On the morning of the scholarship exam I dressed in my best clothes – new stockings and the white jersey I wore only on Sundays. Father had already bought me a new pair of boots; he thought even the pair I wore on Sundays might 'let in' and if the morning turned out wet I might have to sit in the exam room with damp feet. 'That wudn't do, son, wud it?' he said.

We congregated in front of the College of Technology at twenty to nine. We each carried a pencil-case which included two sharpened pencils, a pen and spare nib, and a rubber and a pencil-sharpener in preparation for the ordeal ahead. At ten to nine we moved into the huge building, its wide corridors flanked with cupboards exhibiting all sorts of machinery, and timorously shuffled into the exam room to our numbered desks. The invigilator warned us that any attempt at cheating would result in disqualification, and we began our first paper – English grammar and an essay – on the dot of nine o'clock.

At noon the ordeal was over. We had tackled mathematical problems; had analysed a complicated sentence, parsed words, and written an essay on our favourite hero – mine was on the career of Admiral Nelson; and finally we'd displayed our general knowledge of the world. Exhausted after these intellectual efforts, we left the building talking excitedly, if not hysterically, comparing our answers.

When I returned home I changed at once into my week-day clothes and tried to put the exam out of my mind. When mother asked me how I'd done I told her that I thought I'd done badly.

'How do you know you didn't do well?'

'Because we compared our answers in arithmetic. I got two or three answers wrong out of five, I'm bound to fail.'

'Oh, you'll mebbe do better than you imagine. Anyway I've great faith in you, son – I don't believe you'll fail.'

Father told me the same when he returned from work and, better still, handed me a florin.

'You done yer best, son. You can't do no more nor that, no matter who or what y'are.'

On the following Sunday I called at Portallo Street to give an account of the exam, and then proceeded to Hatfield Street to see uncle Willie and aunt Ida. Grandma Boyd presented me with a shilling and uncle Willie gave me a half-crown; so no matter what the final result might be, my efforts had brought me *some* reward. Everyone comforted me and reminded me of the time lost in hospital. 'It'll be no disgrace if you fail,' aunt Ida said, shaking her head. 'No disgrace at all.'

A month or so later Mr McKee, standing on his stool at the top of the big room, announced the results. The school, he was proud to say, had won four city scholarships and my name – because it came first alphabetically – was the first to be called; and as the four of us walked up to shake hands with the principal, whose pink face was wreathed in a benign smile, everybody began clapping and, to my amazement, some boys dared to stamp their feet. For a moment I thought everybody had gone mad.

'No stamping!' Mr McKee shouted at once. 'Do you want to put us through the floor and into the Girls' below?'

Then the other teachers shook hands with us, and some boys slapped us on the back, and everybody looked proud and the four of us were pleased as punch and couldn't stop smiling. Mr McKee then gave a speech about how hard work brought its rewards and how every boy in attendance at the school could, if he worked hard, bring credit to his teachers. We felt like heroes.

That day nobody was caned and the teachers were in their best humour, making jokes and not working us hard, allowing us to carry on with private reading, which meant we could open our reading books where we liked and read our favourite stories. After a while we began chatting to one another and the teachers didn't seem to mind at all. The rest of the day passed happily; it was easily the proudest day of my life; but what I couldn't understand was how I'd won a scholarship when I'd done so poorly in arithmetic, with two or three wrong answers out of five.

Then I remembered that on the night before the exam I'd been unable to sleep and had prayed that I might pass. My prayer had come true. That was a strange thing to have happened. I couldn't get it out of my head for a long time.

CHAPTER SIX

'Education's easy carried' was a pronouncement I often heard in Portallo Street. Uncle Willie and aunt Ida seemed to regard it as a self-evident truth, and none of the Boyds ever dared to contradict or challenge it, at least not in my presence. I might have questioned it myself if I'd known what it was supposed to mean, but like winning the scholarship, it remained a bit of a puzzle to me. I didn't even know what the word 'education' really meant; all I knew was that Dr Williamson had it because he was a doctor and the Reverend Gregg had it because he was a clergyman; but somehow ordinary people never had a chance of getting it. For education cost a lot of money, more money than working-class families could afford. It meant going to school for another five or six years while other boys were out at work, some as message boys at five shillings a week – dead-end jobs they were called – and some as apprentices in the shipyards. But at least an apprentice had the chance of becoming a tradesman. My fear was that a scholarship might lead me nowhere, a fear shared by father, who repeated for my benefit his belief that the most important thing in life was 'influence'. What 'influence' meant puzzled me; all I knew was that father maintained that he had hardly any – not even in the County Down railway where he'd worked all his life.

The school chosen for me was the Royal Belfast Academical Institution, the only reason for the choice being its convenience: a tram ride brought me almost to its front gates, whereas the other secondary school meant an extra tram ride. I went to Inst in almost complete ignorance of what kind of school it was: all I knew was that no girls were admitted and this fact seemed to me to make it superior to the Methodist College, which was a mixed school. Only one scholarship boy from Mountpottinger chose Methody and I assumed that that was because nobody had told him that girls also went there.

Inst was very different from Mountpottinger. It had a well-kept lawn at the front and a muddy playing field and a bicycle-shed at the back. In the middle, between the main building and the Common Room, lay the quadrangle where hundreds of boys congregated in the morning before dispersing to the various class-rooms and laboratories. Some of the senior boys were called prefects and were in the sixth form, studying for scholarships to universities. Everything was different: pupils travelled to school from all parts of Belfast and from towns like Bangor and Lisburn; and everybody had to wear the school cap which was quartered yellow and black. The new principal, an Englishman, was making Inst more like an English public school by having four houses – Dill, Larmour, Kelvin and Pirrie – with masters in charge of each house. Some of the staff were in favour of these changes and told us that the old school needed a good shaking up: others were of the opinion that the new principal had a lot of fancy ideas that the old school could very well do without. I, as a devotee of the *Magnet,* was of course in favour of the English public school system.

But one innovation did not meet with my approval: the com-pulsory wearing of the bright new cap to and from school. In the mornings I'd stuff it into my bag and put it on only when I reached the City Hall, after having made sure that no prefects were in sight. Coming back from school I wore it as far as the City Hall and then stuffed it into my bag again. The trouble with it was that it attracted attention far too easily: during my first term, when I didn't dare to break the rule, I had to suffer from attacks on it. A rough big lad would come up from behind, grab my cap, tramp on it and run off shouting, 'Who spilt the egg on yer cap?' It was safe enough to wear such a showy cap when you were in town, but not when you were walking along the Albert Bridge Road or Temple-more Avenue. Although the discipline of Mountpottinger had moulded me into being the most timid of conformists, conformity had, in this instance, to give way to commonsense. And as I couldn't run the risk of losing my new cap, the school rule had to be disobeyed. It was the only rule I deliberately flouted.

At Christmas my first report arrived home and caused so much consternation that I would have left Inst if that had been possible. Father read it over and over again, comparing my marks with the average marks of the class and demanding why I'd performed so badly. Most damning of all was the judgement of the principal at the end: 'Very disappointing for a scholarship holder'. Mother, as usual, was much more understanding of my difficulties but, as usual, less than tactful towards father and his puzzlement. To me she said, 'Don't expect your father to know anything about these things', a remark which was not calculated to improve matters between father and me, or between father and herself.

The truth was that we were all out of our depth, myself most of all. Released from the regimentation of Mountpottinger and suddenly given the freedom of Inst, I reacted by completely failing to adapt to my new environment. Inst was a different world. The classrooms were spacious, each of us with a separate desk; most of the masters were friendly and none had canes; in one classroom there was even a lower-form library containing all sorts of adventure and school stories. I was like a prisoner given unexpected liberty and immediately abused it; I did as little homework as possible and went unpunished; I daydreamed in class and found I was ignored; and after school I dawdled home with my cap stuffed in my bag. Once home, bag flung into our parlour, I forgot all about Inst until the next day. I was floundering unhappily between two worlds: the world of Ballymacarett and the world of a middle-class school where the masters came from Oxford and Cambridge, Trinity and Queen's, and the pupils from houses in the suburbs or farms in the country. I found no snobbery, no bullying and no unfriendliness, and I should have been able to settle down to my lessons, make friends and receive good reports at the end of each term. But I became apathetic, remained friendless, and sought refuge in Chatsworth Street and in my old haunts – the public library, the public baths, the Victoria Park, the Oval football ground on Saturday afternoons, the pictures on Saturday nights.

The only building I frequented at Inst was the gym, where I was singled out by the instructor, Sergeant Watkins, for being athletic on the 'horse'. I loved to race to the springboard, bounce high into the air, complete a somersault and land safely on the mat where the watchful sergeant waited.

'You've the makin's of a first-class gymnast, young fella,' the wrinkled sergeant told me, wiping the sweat off his forehead. 'The arms need to be strengthened, but the legs is good, an' the body's trim. Join my extra class.'

I loved going to that gym class, held when lessons were over and the school deserted, apart from a few boys kicking a ball in the back field, or one or two boys riding in front of the bicycle-shed. The sergeant would make us march and run, jump the horse and climb the ropes and bars until we were lathered with sweat and he was breathless. Then he'd dismiss us in his gruff army voice, 'Clear off, boys! Time's up! Away an' do your homework – else you'll get me the sack!'

It took me about two years to feel that I belonged to Inst, and during that time my reports gradually improved. I became interested in chemistry and physics, enjoying the experiments and recording the results in imposing black notebooks. In particular, I loved the sight, smell and atmosphere of the laboratories – the polished wooden benches scarred from previous experiments; the Bunsen burners with their adjustable flames; the beautifully shaped flasks and mysteriously potent bottles which we were taught to handle carefully; the surrounding apparatus in cupboards which whetted our appetite for scientific research.

We respected our master – 'Beaky' Manning – because he kept good discipline without intimidating us. But one master, an Englishman with a rasping, lisping accent, occasionally took the class, and dissipated the relaxed atmosphere with his ill-temper. I still remember his snarling reprimand, 'Boy, where were you bwought up?' He would pause, and a silence would fall over the class who were familiar with what was to follow: 'You weren't bwought up, you were dwagged up from the guttah!' No matter to whom the insult was directed, I wilted under the sting of it, conscious that Lord Street and 'The Gut', and their drunken fights on Friday and Saturday nights weren't far removed from the gutter.

But Inst made no distinction between scholarship holders and the majority of pupils whose parents paid their fees. Indeed those of us with scholarships tended to be favoured; we were expected to bring academic distinction to the school, and many of us did; but some of us – those uninterested in games – were called 'swots'. There was no danger of my being called a swot: I loved all kinds of games – soccer, rugby, cricket, handball – and would spend part of the summer term training for the annual sports held in Osborne Park on the Malone Road. To my surprise and disappointment I discovered I was a poor runner, without speed or stamina, and therefore useless at field events. But I also discovered that I was one of the best cricketers of my age in the school and soon got selected for the third eleven. It was my aptitude for games rather than my academic capability which enabled me to adapt to Inst.

If the repressive atmosphere of Mountpottinger was responsible for my timidity and diffidence, Inst was responsible for increasing my feelings of self-consciousness and social inferiority. Though there was no snobbery at Inst, I was becoming a snob – by which I mean I was more and more conscious of belonging, by birth and upbringing, to what I regarded as an inferior class. I lived in a house and street I was ashamed of, while most of the boys I knew at Inst lived in villas in quiet suburban avenues; my father wore dungarees and worked in the railway, while their fathers were business men, doctors, dentists, architects, teachers, civil servants; and their mothers – whom I'd seen at the Christmas Concert and at Sports' Day – wore expensive-looking clothes and spoke with a semi-English accent.

More and more I withdrew from playing games in Chatsworth Street. No more football with a sixpenny rubber ball or cricket with a bat made from a rough plank and chalk markings on the wall for wickets. Now I played cricket on a prepared grass pitch with a real bat and in white flannels, shirt, and shoes; and instead of playing knock-up football in the muddy 'wee field' I played rugby in proper togs and with the luxury of a shower after the game. The long winter evenings I spent indoors, reading or doing my homework.

I concentrated mainly on my English, history and geography homework partly because I liked those subjects, but even more because I liked the teacher. Mr Greer's classes were supposed to be the most relaxed in the school. If you didn't pay much attention in class, or if you were lax with your homework, Billy – as we all called him – allowed you to go your own way. His passion was scouting, and sometimes he devoted the whole of a forty-minute period discussing the joys of camping with the half dozen scouts in his class. The rest of us contemptuously or enviously referred to these pupils sitting in the front row as Billy's pets. As soon as the class roll was called, one of them would make an inquiry about troop activities and Billy would be diverted from the lesson and the homework to a discussion of some boring scouting topic. The rest of us would spend our time chatting or playing game after game of X's and O's in our jotters. But sometimes Billy would refuse to be diverted and surprise us by announcing to us with a wry smile, 'We're not doing enough work in this class! Let us set to and forget all about scouting!'

He was a small fair-haired fine-featured man with a pleasant smile who, when he devoted himself to teaching, taught with good humour and enthusiasm. He'd the knack of coaxing us to take an interest in far-off countries, in poems such as *The Rime of the Ancient Mariner* or in chivalry during the Middle Ages. His secret, I now believe, was his ability to turn every lesson into a story. His pets said that when he brought them on camping holidays, he loved to gather the troop round the camp-fire so that he could tell them stories about scouts who'd performed deeds of daring. For most of my first year Billy paid little attention to me. But one afternoon, after I'd finished drawing a map, he bent over my shoulder and whispered:

'You're very quiet, aren't you?'

I didn't know what to reply, so kept silent and still, too shy to make any response other than a nod.

'You take great care with your maps, don't you?'

I nodded again.

'I must get to know you better. I know your initial, but not what it stands for.'

I told him.

'I don't like my boys to be too quiet – or too rowdy. Why aren't you a scout?'

I told him that I'd once belonged to a pack of cubs attached to Albert Bridge church.

'Good. Good. Then there's no reason why you shouldn't join our troop. We need recruits. See me after school – if you've nothing to do.'

So I joined the Inst troop, and soon found myself sitting in one of the front desks in Billy's classes, discussing patrols, badges, camping and everything to do with scouting. We were devoted to our scoutmaster, our troop, our school, our country and our flag; above all, perhaps, we were devoted to the romantic challenges of the outdoor life. The camaraderie of scouting was just what I needed, and my admiration for our scoutmaster made me dedicate myself to the subjects he taught. It was the easiest way I could insinuate myself into his favour: for I could summon up no interest in tying knots or passing badges. When the results of the Junior Certificate appeared, I was awarded with marks of distinction in all three of Billy's subjects, and in geography my mark was the highest in Northern Ireland. As Billy's class was only the B section in the form this achievement was regarded as almost miraculous; and when I was asked how I had achieved it, I shrugged and muttered something about the exam papers suiting me and that I'd guessed some of the questions. Billy grasped me warmly round my shoulders, congratulated me and at once gave me promotion in the troop – which was something I didn't desire at all. All I wanted was to bask in his favour without reward and give him my adoration.

To my dismay my academic achievement resulted in my being put into the A class which was taught by the head of the English department, Mr Pyper or 'Johnny', a middle-aged man with a gruff manner who taught conscientiously but whose monotonous voice put me asleep. I respected him, but I was a failure in his class. My marks were never as high again.

More and more I contrived to keep out of our house in Chatsworth Street. Father seemed to be increasingly irritable and was always complaining of mother's neglect of him and her daily trips to Carlton Street, where my young sister was now installed. According to father, this had become mother's real home; he accused her of spending more time there than she did with him; and as for me, he bitterly complained that he hardly ever saw me and that I seldom put my foot in the house except at meal-times and at night. Yet mother, it seemed to me, gave nearly all her time and attention to my younger sister and brother; and father, after his railway work was over, had nothing whatsoever to interest him but would mope about the house before taking himself off to Portallo Street to visit his own parents, brothers and sisters.

Father frequently hinted to me that now I was almost grown up – I was fifteen – it was time that I undertook some responsibility in the running of the house. Things couldn't go on like this much longer. Did I know what was wrong? No, I didn't. Didn't I suspect anything? No, I didn't. What did he mean, I wondered. All he'd say was that something was 'radically wrong', a phrase he'd picked up in the *Belfast Telegraph,* and he couldn't understand how I could live in the house and not notice anything amiss.

Then one day I came home from school to find father threatening to throw mother out, his voice hoarse with anger. 'Here, take yer coat an' get out! Get out! Get out of my sight!'

Father, still wearing his dirty dungarees, held mother's shabby overcoat in his hand and threw it at her as I appeared in the kitchen. Mother, a defiant expression on her face, sat as if sightless, her hair dishevelled.

'What's wrong?' I asked.

'Can't you guess?' father shouted. 'You're a fool if you can't!'

I turned to mother on the sofa. She was examining her old faded blue coat with its torn lining as if it didn't belong to her. She looked ill and tired.

'It's time you an' me had a talk together,' he said to me.

'What's up, father? I don't know what's wrong.'

'If you don't, then it's time you did.'

'Mother's not well. I know that!'

'An' you know what's the matter wi' her, don't you? Luk at the

65

cut of her. . . Is she sober or is she drunk?'

Father suddenly lunged forward, grabbed mother by the shoulders and dragged her upstairs, threatening to kill her as he did so.

'Don't. . . touch. . . me!' mother screamed, trying to grasp the bannister.

I ran into the hall to close the front door, then went into the parlour and sat holding my hands over my ears. Father came downstairs, took out his cigarettes and began smoking. At first he didn't speak, his breath coming in nervous pants. Then at last he said, 'You'll have to know the truth.'

He told me the story of his marriage and how happy he'd been till mother began drinking a year or so after their wedding; and he blamed her mother for encouraging her. He called grandma Leeman a bad old bitch, and said he wished she was in hell, for if anybody deserved to be burning in hell the old woman I called my grandma deserved that fate. He talked for a long time, smoking cigarettes all the while, repeating himself and becoming so incoherent that I could hardly make out what he was saying. At last he broke down and wept. I'd never seen father in tears before, and I could hardly keep back my own tears. We sat quiet for a long time and father at last became calm.

Later I went upstairs. Mother was huddled up in bed, a thin blanket covering her. She was asleep and breathing so quietly that at first I feared she might be dead. Then I tiptoed from the room.

After his confession that day father made me his confessor, so much so that mother accused him of poisoning my mind. At times I hated father for his weakness, and at other times I hated mother for hers. Weeks and months passed. Then father told me we were leaving Chatsworth Street. He'd found a house away from Ballymacarett, in a street not far from his own parents, and he said that mother had seemed pleased when he told her, and had promised to behave better. He had decided to give her another chance. A new house in a new district might bring us some happiness, for we couldn't go on living in the same way.

Father believed that our new house would help mother to reform her habits. The sooner we were out of Chatsworth Street and the temptation of the Lord Street public houses, the better. He told me that for years mother had been drinking steadily, bringing bottles of cheap wine home and hiding them in places where she imagined they would never be found. But he had discovered them, and in the most unlikely places: beneath floorboards in the back room where I slept; on top of the wardrobe in the front room; behind the gas meter in the little cupboard off the kitchen; at the back of the coal-shed in the yard. The wonder was that I'd never found a bottle myself, he said. Did I never search for one? Did I never smell mother's breath? Did I never notice her walking a bit unsteadily? Did I never see her sneak into one of the pubs? Did I never notice how things would suddenly disappear – things like shoes, coats, dresses, blankets, tablecloths? He hardly believed me when I told him that I'd noticed nothing; that I'd never come across a bottle or a pawn-ticket; that I'd never been suspicious of mother's behaviour. Why should I be? I couldn't explain to father that, no matter what he might tell me, I'd go on loving mother. Nothing he said made any difference to me. When they quarrelled I could never take father's part, though I knew he was often in the right.

That day, within the space of a few hours, time accelerated and I was deprived of part of my boyhood.

CHAPTER SEVEN

The new house was number nine Ranelagh Street. It looked raw and damp when we moved in, the back and front garden full of bricks, the pebble-dashed walls not yet dried out. The end of a terrace of four, it struck me as jerry-built and ugly, but as it had a third bedroom as well as an indoor bathroom and lavatory, it suited us well enough. And the small street, lying between a residential avenue and an estate of semi-detached villas built for ex-servicemen of the first world war, certainly appeared to be quieter than Chatsworth Street.

But Ranelagh Street wasn't as quiet as we had hoped it might be. As soon as we moved in we discovered that a mineral-water factory behind the corrugated paling at the back caused a lot of noise; the girls and youths were always yelling and larking as they moved the heavy crates about the yard. Luckily father was on the dayshift at this time and so the noise didn't upset him. It upset me more, and I usually put off doing my homework until I saw the young workers streaming out of the front gate. In a way I envied them their carefree spirits as they worked, hauling the crates of empty bottles across the cemented yard and shouting abuse at one another. At lunch-time the youths played football and the girls in their red rubber aprons applauded or booed until the factory whistle ended the game. At six o'clock, the factory finally fell silent and I could begin my homework in peace.

For a while the flit to Ranelagh Street appeared to be a success. Mother would even accompany father to Portallo Street to prove to the Boyd family how well she was behaving. I loved to see her dressed neatly and full of chat, talking to father's parents as if she hadn't a care in the world. As for father, he radiated happiness and did all he could to make her happy. He had a generous nature; and although he'd over a hundred pounds deposited in the savings

68

bank 'for fear of a rainy day', he'd no great desire to have more. He bought new furniture for the new house so that mother could proudly display it, and he could invite his railway mates home for supper and a game of whist. He bought himself a good second-hand bicycle, because when working the early shift he had to be at the railway before the morning trams began. A bicycle was a necessity now that he lived so far away from the BCDR shunting sheds where he collected his engine. He bought me a bicycle too, because my journey to school was even further than his to work; and my bicycle had to be brand-new so that I wouldn't feel inferior to the other boys. And the very first week we moved into Ranelagh Street he bought mother a new rig-out by way of celebration. Father liked a bit of display, whether it was his own railway jacket with its brass buttons, mother in a good coat and expensive Sunday hat, or myself in my black school blazer and yellow and black cap. Clothes, to him, were the outward sign of a family who had self-respect and desired the respect of their neighbours.

In the past he'd been deeply ashamed of mother – ashamed of her drinking, of her getting into debt, of her running about shabbily dressed – but now he hoped that those days were all over. As uncle Willie and aunt Ida had prophesied more than once to him: 'A new environment will make Jenny into a new woman', and father, though he'd only the vaguest of notions what 'environment' meant, had great faith in their judgment. For about six months mother was as good as gold – proud of her appearance, careful with money, and content to work about the house all day and stay in at night to keep him company.

But our idyllic life wasn't to last: our new environment proved to have disadvantages. Mother, who loved neighbourliness, found that the neighbours didn't run in and out of one another's houses, as in Chatsworth Street, for cups of tea and gossip. Indeed there wasn't any friendliness beyond a 'good morning' or 'lovely day', followed by a front door being firmly closed. And there were no grocery shops handy where she could make new friends. She had to go as far as the shops on the Woodstock Road; and once free of the house, she was tempted to take a tram to Mountpottinger and call in at Carlton Street. In any case she considered it was only right that she should call – my young sister still lived there, as it was so near to her school.

One day a letter arrived for father from McDowell's shop in Lord Street saying that mother had left owing them twenty-seven pounds.

'What does this mean, Jenny?' father shouted, waving the bit of paper.

Mother, who had given her word that she'd left Chatsworth Street with all of her debts paid, burst into tears and admitted that she'd told an untruth, that she was sorry for what she'd done, and that she'd pay off every penny as soon as she could.

To my surprise, father controlled his temper and handed over the bill in silence. He turned to me, and said sadly, 'What can I do? What can I do?'

But I'd no comfort to offer him and he went to his bedroom, his face very pale, as if stunned by mother's betrayal.

'There's nothing to worry about,' mother told me, putting the bill into her little purse. 'Mrs McDowell trusts me. She knows I'll pay back every penny I owe her.'

She had deceived father, and I was certain she was now deceiving herself.

'You can't deceive me,' I said, as bitterly as I could. 'You can't deceive me any more.' From now on I'd no choice but to be father's ally: and that brought me little comfort.

Mother took to going to bed early, sometimes as early as eight o'clock or a quarter past, pleading a headache and not feeling well. On these occasions father and I would sit in front of the fire, whispering about her together and hoping that she would be asleep. But she surprised us once by coming downstairs for a glass of water and saying as she stood on the stairs on her way up again: 'You two want me out of the way. So I'm keeping out of your way. And I know what you're saying about me.'

It was true: we discussed her endlessly, wondering what could be done. Father was in despair. He thought mother was drinking again, and if she was he could no longer prevent her. He was beaten, and no one could give him any help. All the efforts he'd made had been in vain, and he confessed that without my support he couldn't go on. We discussed what could be done even though he had by now accepted that little *could* be done. All he could do was give mother less money on a Friday night and pay McDowell's bill himself – else it would never be paid. Mother was incapable of keeping her promises. There was no question of that.

So in trying not to fail father, I failed mother. Mother, who needed my help all the more, was denied it. The guilt is with me still.

The house in Ranelagh Street was cold and comfortless in winter, with draughts so strong that they lifted the mats off the floor in the living room; but in summer a cool breeze would invade all the rooms and the front and back gardens gave a feeling of space and light. Nevertheless it was a dreary little street, bereft of character, though it pleased me well enough, especially after the arrival of the hammock.

The hammock was the only present I ever received from granda Leeman, and how he got hold of it I never discovered. On one of my rare visits to Carlton Street he'd told me how well he'd slept on a hammock during a trial voyage up the Scottish coast, and mother assured me that granda would be able to find one for me, though he protested that it wasn't possible as no shops in Belfast sold them. But mother insisted that with so many ships sailing in and out of the lough granda could go down to the docks and at least make inquiries.

I've no idea what inquiries were in fact made, but granda turned up one Saturday morning with the hammock wrapped round his shoulders like an old shawl and the pair of us put it up in the back garden. Third or fourth hand at least, it looked as if it had swung on the forecastle of many ships. When I scrambled into it I realised why sailors preferred it to a bed: it was more comfortable than any bed I'd ever slept in. Every fine day during the summer I would hitch it up, read my books and lie luxuriating in the sun. Father, on arriving home after work, would shake his head and tartly remark, 'It's well to be some people that can take life aisy.' Clearly the fear that he might be bringing up an educated loafer

71

was troubling his mind, and how could I blame him? I was greedy for education but my notion of education had nothing to do with hard work, at least not as father knew it.

Life was becoming easier for me at school. At last, after three years, I'd settled down at Inst, was enjoying the classes and the games, and had gained entry into the senior school. It was a cocooned life, and everything outside the gates of the school seemed irrelevant and insignificant. We ignored the sporadic 'troubles' between Catholics and Protestants as long as they didn't impinge on our activities. At home politics were of little interest; father, who cycled through the Short Strand on his way to the railway, always had a good word for Catholics: 'No Catholic ever harmed me, that's all I've got to say about them.' And uncle Willie, engaged in his trade-union affairs, had no time for bigotry: 'My job is to bring workers together, not to keep them apart.' As for aunt Ida, she never missed an opportunity to talk about socialism to anyone who'd listen to her; but being childless she would be pooh-poohed as a bit of an oddity: better if she paid more attention to the needs of her husband than to matters that didn't concern her. The Boyd family held the opinion that my aunt Ida gabbled far too much for a woman, did no housework, and wasted her time at political meetings when she should have busied herself at home. As for myself, I must have been born a socialist; for every argument aunt Ida and uncle Willie advanced seemed to me logical and irrefutable. I'd already thought of them myself, being a natural equalitarian. When I read Bernard Shaw's *The Intelligent Woman's Guide to Socialism and Capitalism* in 1928, when it first appeared, I was surprised to learn that Shaw had shamelessly borrowed many of his ideas from my uncle and aunt.

They were my favourite relations, and more and more I gravitated to their house on Sundays after I'd attended the Sunday school belonging to Albert Bridge Congregational Church. Father still went to church every Sunday, taking his pew in the gallery and dutifully paying his free-will offering, which he noted in the annual accounts to be larger than that donated by worshippers better off than himself. Mother seldom accompanied him, her

72

excuse being that he sang so out of tune that she found the service painful. But this was only an excuse: mother's restlessness extended to religion and she liked to please herself concerning what service, if any, she attended. Under the influence of Mrs McClune and Mrs McIlroy, two Chatsworth Street neighbours, she attended the Elim Tabernacle, but, unlike her neighbours, she refused to be 'born again' despite the potent persuasiveness of the evangelist. Of course father would have been in favour of mother's 'conversion', though he'd no time himself for preachers threatening the everlasting torture of hellfire. Nor had mother, who had her own tortures. She enjoyed the singing of the hymns, the lively ones in particular; if the prayers and the sermons had been left out she'd have raised no objection.

My own interest in religion was never intense, even in childhood. I'd been accustomed to kneel at my bedside to say the Lord's Prayer and ask for blessings, but as I grew older my prayers became more perfunctory, and sometimes, on cold nights, I hopped into bed without kneeling down, and once I was warmly tucked in under the bedclothes, my prayers were forgotten. As I seemed to come to no harm my habit of prayer gradually ceased, though I continued my attendance at Sunday school because I liked the company of our little group there. I've no idea how Sunday schools are conducted nowadays, but I hope they haven't changed too much since I attended Albert Bridge Congregational Sunday School where we sang a couple of hymns for children and prayed a little, but spent most of the hour listening to stories from the Bible. These stories I loved, and I enjoyed the singing, but the prayers bored me. It was a pleasant Sunday school, with young teachers and an easy-going atmosphere. Best of all you were given a book as a prize for good attendance throughout the year, and we would also spend a day by the seaside in summer, an excursion by train to Bangor, Donaghadee or Newcastle. If the weather was wet it would be a disaster, but if it was dry it would be a treat — with buns, cups of tea, lemonade, races, sand and sea. These Sunday school prizes were the first books I ever owned. When a couple of them turned out to be pious tales I persuaded my teacher to allow me to make my own choice, and selected a couple of adventure stories which I re-read for years. So Sunday school was entirely satisfactory as far as I was concerned. Its only drawback was that it was held only once a week.

But Sunday school also accelerated my disbelief; one member of the class, a boy called Johnny Smyth, refused to believe in miracles and told our teacher they were silly stories. I agreed with him, but lacked the courage to follow his lead. We soon became friends and, instead of going to Sunday school, we would meet outside and walk across the Albert Bridge and along the Sand Quay to the Custom House steps to listen to the various speakers there – the lay theologians interpreting the Bible, the politicians preaching socialism and the quacks selling patent medicines. This was another kind of education, and one I preferred to what I was given at Mountpottinger, or even in Sunday school. The debates on the Custom House steps produced some sharp and robust repartee which greatly amused us: and more importantly, we learnt to listen to speeches and not to accept them at their face value. In short, we learnt the value of scepticism. It was my first encounter with a crude form of dialectics, and I understood why Johnny had come to question our young Sunday school teacher's belief in biblical miracles.

One of the legacies from my Mountpottinger days was an excessive fear of teachers. Though most Inst teachers were good-humoured, there were a few whose tantrums frightened me so much that I learnt nothing in their classes. In the Latin class, for instance, I sat as if petrified, waiting to be singled out to translate a passage from Caesar's *Gallic Wars* – a text I found almost incomprehensible; and when I *was* able to decipher a sentence it proved to be so commonplace that it held no interest at all for me. Even worse I was subjected to questioning about monstrosities called the dative and ablative case. This language and its teacher terrified me. From the first day in the class when we learnt to decline *mensa,* to the end of the second year when we'd tortuously worked our way through a detestable chocolate-coloured Latin grammar full of conjugations and declensions, I spent hours and hours of wasted time that seemed to stretch into eternity, hours spent in such a state of nervous tension that my stomach was knotted and my head ready to burst. Incapable of learning anything I was relegated to the bottom of the class and judged to have no ability for languages, for the same teacher took me for both Latin and French, and I was ordered to give up Latin and demoted to the lowest section of the form for French. Later, with sympathetic teachers, I took up both languages again; and many years later I came to know my Latin master and found him to be a sensitive and cultured man with a wide knowledge of classical and modern literature. But, as a young teacher without patience and with an uncontrollable temper, he was responsible for alienating hundreds of boys from his subjects, and though I came to admire his scholarship, I never forgot or forgave the hours of torture I endured in his classroom.

Fortunately I liked many of the Inst masters. I think one of my favourites was a dapper little Frenchman, Monsieur Carré, who, for one period a week, took an extra class devoted to reading short stories. The purpose of this class was to improve our accent and widen our vocabulary. As our accent was execrable and our vocabulary meagre, Monsieur Carré had a daunting task, so daunting indeed that his sharp features often winced at our attempts to speak his native language. After my previous failure at French I was determined to prove that this hadn't been my fault and I decided to take advantage of having a real Frenchman as my teacher. Consequently I sat immediately in front of Monsieur Carré, concentrating on every word he spoke and trying to imitate his accent. I even took the trouble of looking up in *Le Nouveau Petit Larousse* all the unfamiliar words that occurred in the stories. Then, having written the synonyms in pencil in the margin of my copy of the stories, I delighted Monsieur Carré with the apparent richness of my vocabulary and my enthusiasm to contribute to the *explication de texte*. I also impressed him by my attempts to improve my accent. As a reward he recommended me to Mr Harriman, head of the modern languages department, as a most promising and eager student of French who should be promoted from the lowest section of the form to the highest. Never was virtue, allied to subterfuge, given such welcome recognition. I reached the conclusion that schoolmasters, whom I'd regarded as exemplars of intellect, could also be remarkably naive. Much more important, I satisfied myself that I'd some aptitude for foreign languages and asked permission to start Spanish. Inst was like that: a trier would be encouraged. If the staff contained a few incompetent and lazy teachers the majority taught conscientiously and competently; and, best of all, with good humour.

CHAPTER EIGHT

Once admitted to the senior school I rapidly gained confidence; I joined societies, haunted the reference library, and participated in the school plays – always by Shakespeare, and performed near Christmas. I wasn't much good as an actor and was given small parts, though my Portia in *Julius Caesar* brought me the praise I hungered for. But the part I was given never bothered me, indeed the smaller the part the better pleased I was, for all I wanted was to be included in the production – prompter, actor, general factotum, hanger-on – what matter? I was stage struck at sixteen; and Inst introduced me to the excitement of drama. I couldn't have wished for a better introduction. We thought our productions brilliant – and they may have been; I've no means of judging how good or bad they were, and I don't think the standard we reached really matters. We enjoyed ourselves, and the staff, who contributed as producers, stage-managers, electricians and designers, were proud of us (and of themselves). The audiences, mostly parents and relations, gave us enthusiastic receptions, and a good time was had by all, which is after all the purpose of drama. Our casts were all male, or to be more precise, all adolescent, and none of us, I remember, liked being given· female roles. I certainly didn't, and had to be persuaded to take the part of Portia. I don't imagine my performance was a very convincing one because my voice was in the process of breaking. I hated having to wear skirts and two rolled-up rugby socks across my chest; they would refuse to stay in place, and my fellow actors would insist on squeezing and patting them. I'd never a high opinion of myself as an actor, and the embarrassment I'd to endure playing Portia almost put me off acting for good.

But while at Inst I'd the rare opportunity of appearing on the professional stage. The stage was that of the Belfast Opera House, and the occasion was the annual visit of the Frank Benson Company. Extras were required in the Shakespeare productions and were supplied by various amateur companies including our own. The only qualification was to be of a reasonable height and as I was less than five and a half foot tall, I wasn't at first selected. It was only when somebody dropped out through illness and I volunteered to be a replacement that I managed to persuade our master to give me my chance. And when we took up our positions on the Opera House stage, greatness was thrust upon me, because instead of being in the back row of the extras I was put in the front – else I would have been invisible to the audience. The consequence was that I got a very close view of the professionals at work, indeed so close that I would forget to move when I had to, and once or twice I had a spear stuck in my behind to remind me to move. The whole experience intoxicated me: the pungent smell of make-up, the richness of Shakespearean speech, the gay colours of Elizabethan costume, the glare of the footlights, the laughter and applause of the audience, the swish of the heavy velvet curtain at the end of each act. And of course I fell in love with one of the principal actresses, a small lissom young woman whose every gesture and syllable made me almost swoon with delight. As for the great Sir Frank Benson himself, I considered him far too decrepit to play opposite my paragon. Admittedly his face had nobility and his speech resonance, but to my jealous eyes his knees were knobbly, his legs thin, and his gestures forced and unnatural. Perhaps my low opinion of myself as an actor had been too severe, and there was a possibility after all that I might have talent. So I permitted myself to lead a fantasy life with my heroine, playing Hamlet to her Ophelia until the Benson fortnight ended, the players departed, the magic faded and we stage-struck extras were bumped back to earth and the realities of classrooms, exams and rugby games.

When I told aunt Ida of my histrionic exploits she was delighted and clapped her hands. She was always urging me to 'widen my horizons' – to use her own phrase. Aunt Ida was a great one for getting hold of a phrase and working it to death; she liked to dramatise too and if there was a mirror in the room she peered at herself as she mouthed the phrase over. In socialist circles she'd gained a reputation as an impassioned public speaker, and when offering me advice she'd a habit of gazing far beyond me, perhaps to her imaginary audience. I used to think at that time that if she'd been blessed with a good figure she'd have made a professional actress, but unfortunately she was thin and flat all over and completely lacking in sex appeal. Both she and uncle Willie loved plays, but 'only if they have something important to say'. They considered trivial comedies that titillated the public to be a lamentable waste of time. So they brought me to the pit of the Opera House to see Sybil Thorndike in *Saint Joan* and the Abbey Players in *Juno and the Paycock*. *Saint Joan* interested me: *Juno* enthralled me. It is from those productions that I date my admiration of Shaw and my love of O'Casey.

Besides bringing me to 'serious' plays, my aunt and uncle lent me 'serious' books, including the Webbs' *History of Trade Unionism* which, though of absorbing interest to them, was unreadable to me, for then, as now, I read mostly for pleasure. But I dipped into their collection of socialist and radical literature and found some novels and essays which were more to my taste: novels by Upton Sinclair and Sinclair Lewis, essays by Robert Blatchford and James Connolly. And it was from aunt Ida and uncle Willie that I first heard of Marx and Engels – and of W.B. Yeats. I didn't borrow Marx from them then, but I did borrow Yeats's *Early Poems and Stories*.

I can hardly remember a time when I couldn't read. The only books at home were a couple of Bibles and hymn books and half a dozen volumes of *Studies in the Bible* which father was cajoled into buying at the doorstep from an evangelist. But I was fortunate enough to have access to libraries, either private or public; and long before I could afford to buy my own books I bought them second hand, usually in Smithfield, and walked home with one or two under my arm, preferring to spend my pocket money on a copy of Ruskin's *Sesame and Lilies* than on a tram or bus fare.

At Inst the balance between an interest in learning and an interest in games was well maintained, and as a senior I'd a foot in both worlds. More and more I frequented the library, so much so that 'Beaky' Manning, my old science master who was in charge, appointed me as one of his assistants. Nothing could have pleased me more; and at every opportunity – lunch-time, during a free period, or for an hour or so after school – I'd rush up the stairs to select a book and settle down to read at the large rectangular table. That high silent room, with its view of the front lawn, school gates and tennis courts, was for me a kind of eyrie, comfortable and consoling, where by the simple act of picking up a book and becoming absorbed in it, I could escape from any unhappiness at home or stress at school. Sometimes Beaky – the first bibliophile I ever met – would draw my attention to a recent acquisition. He'd handle the book carefully, as if it were a precious vase, wiping it with a soft, yellow cloth, and blowing away any specks of dust hidden behind the spine, and then he'd present it for my inspection.

'That's the first volume of Skeat's great edition of Chaucer. It's just come into the library, so I hope to find an enthusiast for Geoffrey Chaucer. How about yourself?'

'I wouldn't have enough time, sir.'

'Ah, of course not. Exams must be passed, I suppose. I'm sorry you dropped science, young man. Now why on earth did you do that? Was it because you are by way of being a literary fellow and therefore a despiser of science? I hope not, but I fear so.'

Beaky had a deeply resonant voice which he seldom had occasion to raise, but whenever he did, it reverberated far beyond the walls of the library; and if he caught a boy mishandling any of his beloved books the miscreant would be given such a tirade that he'd never dare repeat the offence, and probably never dare enter the library again.

It was Beaky, I imagine, who first put a book of Forrest Reid's into my hand with the words he often used: 'You may find that to your taste, young man.'

I did find this book very much to my taste. It was called *Apostate*. I looked up the word in the dictionary and when I discovered its meaning I realised that I too could claim to be an apostate. Forrest Reid and I had at least this in common: neither of us could accept orthodox Christianity. I can still remember the pleasure I derived from a sentence like this: 'I hated Sunday, I hated church, I hated Sunday school, I hated Bible stories, I hated everybody mentioned in both the Old and New Testaments, except perhaps the impenitent thief, Eve's snake, and a few similar characters.' I relished the hammer-like blows of Forrest Reid's hatred, though my own feelings were very different from his: I had liked Sunday school, I had liked the Bible stories, particularly those, like Naaman the leper, cured by bathing in the Jordan, Joseph and his coat and David and Goliath, in the Old Testament; and my main feeling about church was that the service went on too long and bored me. But I didn't hate it.

Apostate was the first autobiography I ever read and I'm glad I read it while I was still at Inst, Forrest Reid's old school. When I told Beaky that I'd enjoyed *Apostate*, he nodded his head gravely and protruded his lower lip, signs that he himself had reservations and couldn't altogether share my enthusiasm. I wondered why, but he never offered any explanation. *Apostate* was a revelation to me: here was a writer who, like myself, belonged to Inst; a writer who described what the school was like in his day, and who actually described parts of Belfast (though the scenes of his upbringing in the university area were unfamiliar to me); above all, a writer who shared the thoughts and understood the desires of a schoolboy like myself. Identifying with the young Forrest, I felt as if the book had been especially written for me, even if the middle-class background wasn't mine – indeed his world of governesses and day nurseries was completely foreign to me. But such differences mattered hardly at all. *Apostate* described a boy growing up in Belfast, and as I was doing precisely that, this was the book for me. Beaky, in one of our brief chats about Forrest Reid, did admit that *Apostate* was well written.

'Oh yes, yes, yes,' he remarked, sitting in his chair at the window, twiddling his thumbs, his pudgy hands over his waistcoat, 'a stylist, no doubt about that. But a strange fellow, all the same. . . Very odd fellow. . . yes, yes, no doubt about it.' But as I thought Beaky himself a bit odd, in a different way of course, I paid no heed to this judgement. Possibly he thought me odd as well. Anyway we got on well together and he suggested that I might like to try some of Forrest Reid's novels. 'They may well be to your taste,' he added drily. And they were. Novels like *Following Darkness, Spring Song* and *Pirates of the Spring* are about boyhood and youth and are best appreciated, I imagine, by the young; the reason being that Forrest Reid was intellectually and emotionally arrested in adolescence. The latent theme of pederasty was never far below the surface of his work. But this I was incapable of understanding at the time, being myself an adolescent and emotionally very immature. Which is of course why these novels appealed to me. Discovering them was the most exciting literary experience of my youth; just as, much later, meeting and becoming friendly with Forrest Reid was one of the most enriching experiences of my adult life. We never became intimate friends – our temperaments were too different for that – but he confided some of his problems to me, including the greatest problem that many of the old and unmarried have to face: loneliness. Though he'd a number of friends in Belfast, Forrest often spent evenings by himself playing patience or playing his gramophone. He had no wireless, bought no newspapers and lived alone. What sustained him was the art he practised until almost the last year of his life.

Because Forrest had attended Inst – without making any mark in scholarship or games – the school reference library had placed his books in a section labelled 'Instoniana', where a heterogeneous collection of works written by Old Boys was always on display. When I'd read all his novels I began on his critical books, attracted most by his study of W.B. Yeats. Curious, that aunt Ida, whose taste was undeveloped and uncertain (as I patronisingly thought) and Forrest Reid, whose taste was sophisticated and highly literary, should both lead me to read Ireland's greatest poet. Before I left Inst I'd immersed myself in Yeats's prose, plays and poetry. He was the subject of the first serious essay (an effusive effort published in the *School News*) that I ever wrote; and when I was invited to belong to an exclusive sixth-form literary club which met monthly at a master's house at Knock, Yeats was the subject of the first paper I delivered. That my paper was mostly lifted from Forrest's book apparently passed unnoticed and it was given undeserved praise. But I remember that a paper on Edmund Burke by a boy younger than myself astonished us all: the prodigy was R.B. McDowell, who later became one of Ireland's best known historians, devoting his life to the period he was already mastering as a schoolboy.

It was therefore by chance that in my last couple of years at Inst I began to immerse myself in Irish writers and wished that I'd a knowledge of Gaelic. I began to wonder too why my education was so one-sided, with all things Irish ignored and all things English lauded. Certainly I didn't feel in the least bit English, and was delighted when Ireland defeated England at rugby, for it was only on such occasions that my latent sense of *patria* could be openly demonstrated. I've already mentioned that Inst, with its English principal and its young masters from English universities, was changing its character during the late 1920s, possibly influenced by the political climate following on the partition of Ireland. Although I'd never met a Catholic of my own age, somebody – probably aunt Ida – told me that Catholic schools were very different from other schools in that Irish language, history and culture were encouraged there, which was something aunt Ida certainly approved of. But uncle Willie – anti-clerical as he was – was strongly of the opinion that no priests or clergymen should be allowed to have anything to do with education. He thought that Inst was the most progressive school in Northern Ireland because no religious instruction was given, and the pupils included Roman Catholics and Jews as well as Protestants.

Not surprising, therefore, that when I thought of my own religious education – which I very seldom did – the few ideas I had were far from clear. Anyway I'd too many other, more pressing matters agitating my mind. Father was still worried that, with every passing year, I was disqualifying myself from more and more jobs. The only job I seemed fitted for was that of librarian, but as jobs in libraries were few and far between, he was almost certain I was heading for permanent unemployment. He was all for my getting as much education as possible, but it seemed to him that I was quite willing to spend a whole lifetime in getting it.

Although games weren't compulsory at Inst you were considered an outsider if you didn't play at least one, preferably rugby; failing rugby, then cricket or rowing; and failing them, tennis. I was willing to play any game – including handball and rounders, but by the time I'd reached the senior forms I'd settled for rugby in winter and cricket in summer. I was soon representing the school in both, playing scrum-half for the third fifteen and as an all-rounder for the second eleven. My prowess at sport brought me status and I spent most of my leisure on the playing fields. I loved Osborne Park with its soft green pitches partly sheltered by tall trees and its cream, pebble-dashed pavilion where we changed, enjoyed the luxurious hot and cold showers, and dressed, our skin pink and tingling and our damp hair combed back. Then I'd cycle homewards along the Malone Road with its large villas where some of the boys lived; down the hill of the Old Stranmillis Road; along by the Lagan and over the river to the Ravenhill Road with its golf course, and finally along the side of the Ormeau Park towards home.

It was a game of rugby at Osborne that changed my life at Inst. I've forgotten who our opponents were, and the match itself is of no importance. Scrum halfs are often small agile players whose position at the base of the scrums puts them into rough physical contact with the opposing forwards who are usually hefty players good at scrummaging. Once, trying to gather the ball from a scrum, I was given a sharp kick on the ankle from an opposing forward, and retaliated by shouting, 'Damn you!' The referee at once blew his whistle and awarded a penalty to the opposition. But before allowing the game to be restarted he demanded to know who'd been guilty of shouting abuse at an opponent. I confessed to the crime, a confession that brought me to the attention of the referee and led to a friendship with him which lasted until his sudden death about a year and a half later.

The referee was George Edward Laurie, head of the classics department, who had the reputation of being the strictest disciplinarian in the school. One of the first questions I remember being asked as a junior was, 'Are you in Laurie's Latin class?' And when I said, 'No', the comment was, 'You're lucky you aren't!' So whenever I saw this fearsome master jauntily striding across the quadrangle, his pince-nez slightly awry across his nose, his sallow face unsmiling, his baggy trousers hitched high to reveal his rumpled socks, I stared at him as he passed me, frightened at the very sight of him and thankful that I'd the good luck not to have to face him daily in his classroom. Other than his reputation, I knew nothing about him, except that he was an enthusiastic referee of rugby games. This was my first encounter with him.

After the game he barked at me: 'Come to my classroom at three o'clock on Monday.' He then turned his back, lifted his muddy boots and strode out of the pavilion, his face grim. Relieved at his disappearance, the rest of the team offered me their condolences, which only increased my foreboding.

'Hard cheese!'

'Bad luck!'

'A bloody terror, oul' Laurie!'

'He'll murder you!'

'God, but you're in for it on Monday!'

'Don't turn up!'

'He'll not forget about you!'

On Monday at three o'clock I entered Mr Laurie's classroom. He sat at his desk, reading. I stood at the door, waiting for him to notice me. I waited for a long time. At last he raised his head.

'Come here.'

I walked slowly across the room and stood in front of his desk, waiting for an explosion of anger. I didn't dare look up but kept my eyes on the floor and tried to prevent myself from trembling. I could hear his breathing. Again he kept silent for what appeared to me a very long time.

'Well?' he said softly.

'Yes, sir.' I could think of nothing else to say.

'Well?' he repeated. 'Are you sorry?'

'Yes, sir.'

'Thank you. The incident is now closed.'

I waited for him to dismiss me, but instead he turned his attention to his book. Then, without looking at me, he spoke, his voice evenly pitched and without emotion.

'On Saturdays at six o'clock two or three senior boys come to my house for tea. Would you like to join us?'

This invitation was so unexpected that I didn't know what to reply; so to give me time he explained what would happen if I chose to accept. Tea would be prepared by his sister who was unmarried and shared his home. After tea there'd be chat and games – nothing very exciting – but if I'd nothing better to do on Saturdays his sister and himself would welcome my company.

'Perhaps we'll see you next Saturday, but if not. . .' He made a slight gesture. 'If not, no harm's done. But come only if you wish to. And please ask your parents' permission if you decide to accept our invitation.'

He dismissed me and I walked slowly to the shed to collect my bicycle, wondering how I could refuse. The last thing on earth I wished was to spend Saturday evenings with old Laurie and two or three of his pets. I was scared of him and didn't know who the other boys might be, probably swots studying classics, and I'd no interest in them or in Latin and Greek, and I wanted nothing to do with old Laurie. Anyway, why had he invited me? That I just couldn't understand. I could imagine no reason at all. It was stupid and I'd have nothing to say to anyone and the evening would be entirely wasted. But how could I refuse without getting into more trouble?

At home all I divulged was that a master had invited some senior boys to tea and would it be all right if I went. Nothing I ever did caused mother any surprise, and she merely said that she hoped I'd have a nice evening. As for father, he was curious to know why a schoolmaster who taught boys from Monday to Friday would want to see them on a Saturday evening. But of course I could do what I liked. . .

I turned up at the house in Bawnmore Road at exactly six o'clock. As I'd been a little early I'd cycled up and down the avenue twice before I summoned up enough courage to push my bicycle through the little gate. I rang the bell and a senior boy came to the door.

'Hello, you're just in time. G.E.L. says put your bike anywhere you like. I left mine at the side of the house.' I did the same and followed him in, noting that the boy – taller and a year or two senior to myself – referred to old Laurie by his initials.

'Ah, take a pew,' G.E.L. said, pointing to an empty chair.

'You weren't at Osborne this afternoon?'

'No, sir.'

'You missed a good game.' Then he turned his attention to the others. 'Yes, we were a trifle lucky to win. If that drop goal of theirs had gone over we'd have lost. Because when our full-back. . .'

During the discussion of the first fifteen's match a small portly middle-aged woman appeared at the door of the sitting-room to announce that tea was now ready, and we all trooped into the dining-room still discussing the victory.

At nine o'clock we left, and as I cycled home I reflected on what had happened since six o'clock. The three hours had passed quickly and I was surprised how much I'd enjoyed myself. G.E.L. – as I now thought of him – had hardly spoken to me, but that I didn't mind in the least; and only one of the boys, called Simon, had chatted to me during tea. Simon was in my own form, but I'd never spoken to him before. He was studying Greek and Latin and was in G.E.L.'s top classes, which was something I didn't envy him at all. He told me he'd tried to play rugby but had been useless and had given it up. The other two boys present played for the second fifteen but he supposed I knew that. I did and told him the positions they played in, but he wasn't interested in what I was saying though I noticed he expected me to be interested when he was talking. I didn't care for him but didn't dislike him either. The other two boys I respected because they played for the seconds. G.E.L. was in good humour all evening, smiling and telling jokes and discussing rugby and cricket matches. Finally we played a card game, using cards with letters to make up words, with G.E.L. acting as arbiter, holding three large dictionaries on his lap. When we parted at the front gate G.E.L. thanked me for coming and hoped I had enjoyed myself.

That winter I spent most of my Saturday evenings at Bawnmore Road. The routine never altered: tea, chat, a game. And we always left together at nine o'clock. I don't really know why I continued going, except that I'd nothing better to do and was afraid of offending G.E.L. During the week I never saw him except when we met accidentally in the quadrangle. Then he'd greet me with a slight smile and a curt 'Hello' and pass on, his sallow face grim. In school he seemed to be a completely different person from our host in his home, where he was always relaxed and happy. What puzzled me was why he'd picked me out as one of his pets, especially as I'd no interest in Greek and Latin. But after a while I never thought any more about this but accepted it.

To be one of G.E.L.'s pets clearly had its advantages. Towards the end of the rugby season I found myself promoted from the third to the second fifteen; and at the beginning of the cricket season I'd a place in the first eleven. In both teams I performed reasonably well, but I was fairly certain that if I hadn't been a 'Laurie pet' I wouldn't have gained these promotions so easily.

Once I fell ill with flu and was absent from school for a week or so. I was still confined to bed when mother came up to my room.

'A gentleman's here to visit you,' she said primly and a little proudly. 'He's downstairs waiting. I'll have to bring him up.'

'Who is he?'

'I didn't get his name. Better straighten up your bed it's that untidy. . . and the state of your room!'

It was G.E.L. I don't know which of us was the more embarrassed when mother left us alone. G.E.L. stood at the side of my bed without taking off his raincoat which he always left unbuttoned. He asked me how I was and hoped I'd soon be back at school. That was all. Without smiling or saying anything more he left. Then mother reappeared, having tidied her hair and put on a fresh apron, but too late.

'Who was that?'

I told her.

'I thought it might be him, but I wasn't sure. And I never even offered him a cup of tea. What'll he think of us? Your father's still hiding in the scullery.'

Then mother went on to explain and complain that father had behaved as usual and left her to cope with a stranger. For father, having peeped through the curtains to make certain it wasn't the insurance man, hadn't the courage to appear and introduce himself and had retreated into the scullery.

'It's well I was in,' she said. 'Your father wouldn't have been able to entertain the gentleman.'

'But we didn't have to entertain him, mother. You say you didn't even offer him tea.'

'No, I didn't. But that wasn't my fault. I could see he wanted out as quick as he could.'

I could understand why. Our house was usually untidy on a Saturday morning, especially if father had been working overtime on Friday and was enjoying a lie-in and a late breakfast. The table hadn't even been cleared when G.E.L. called, and the smell of father's fry was still around the house. Added to that, I was ashamed of my own untidy and shabby bedroom.

'Why did he call anyway?' father was anxious to know. 'Did he imagine you were mitchin'?'

'No. He called to see how I was, father.'

'But why, if it was none of his business you were absent?'

That was a question I couldn't answer.

During the summer term I saw little of G.E.L. except when he was umpiring one of the first eleven games at Osborne Park, or when he accompanied our team to an away game at Armagh or Enniskillen or Dungannon. As an umpire G.E.L. was unpopular with us owing to his shortsightedness: if the visiting eleven made a strong appeal for leg-before-wicket their appeal was nearly always upheld on the grounds that visiting teams should be afforded the benefit of the doubt. Naturally we didn't share G.E.L.'s notion of sportsmanship. So when he turned up to umpire a match we used to groan and mutter that we hadn't a chance of winning because the other team now had a twelfth man playing for them. As the games lasted until fairly late in the evening G.E.L. seldom invited us round to his home. But one Saturday, when a game finished early, he invited me by myself, explaining that he'd a special reason for doing so.

'I've arranged to spend my summer holidays in north Cornwall,' he said as soon as we'd sat down in his sitting-room. 'I'm going to a place called Newquay. I've already invited the others to accompany me for the month of July. We hope to swim, play tennis and explore Cornwall. Would you care to come along with us?'

He explained that I should require the permission of my parents, who would be responsible for my travelling expenses; but that everything else would be his responsibility – the cost of the boarding house, the excursions and all incidental expenses. He regretted being unable to afford my travelling expenses, and if my parents had already made plans for the summer holidays he would of course understand. . .

As usual I got my way: father bought me the concessionary 'privilege' ticket which halved the travelling fare; mother thought the holiday the chance of a lifetime. So, on the day following the end of the summer term, our little party of five – four boys and G.E.L. – met at the Liverpool boat. Father carried my small case as far as the sheds, but as soon as he caught sight of our party (some of the other boys had also brought a parent along) he handed over the case.

'I'll go no further. Mind an' have a good holiday. An' forget all about. . .everything. . .while you're away. You've enough money wi' you, haven't ye? But if ye run short, don't forget to write an' tell me. . . I'll send you the necessary. . . Don't stint yerself in any way, mind.' With a gulped 'Cheerio now' he left the sheds.

CHAPTER NINE

I spent my seventeenth birthday in Cornwall, far from home for the first time and in the company of three boys I didn't know well and a master I hardly knew at all. It was one of the best holidays I've ever spent, and one of the strangest. First of all, G.E.L. behaved throughout as if he were an older brother and not a middle-aged schoolmaster noted for his strict discipline in the classroom. I can remember his appearance at breakfast in the dining room of our boarding house overlooking the sea. He dressed casually, wearing an open-necked white shirt, grey flannels (too short as usual), and a pair of black unpolished shoes. While the four of us chatted he read *The Times*, occasionally lifting his head to inform us that Hobbs had scored a century for Surrey or Hendren for Middlesex. Then he'd fold his newspaper and inquire how we proposed to spend the day. We usually split up into twos and threes: seldom did all five of us keep together, except for tennis. On Sunday mornings G.E.L. would let it be known that he was setting out for church, and usually a couple of us would go with him. But, like everything else, attendance at church was voluntary, and throughout the month I attended only once. I wish I'd attended more often, for the beauty of the little Cornish church still remains with me.

During that month of July it seemed to all four of us that G.E.L. was as happy as ourselves. We never discussed his character. Certainly the notion of homosexuality was never mentioned, and I couldn't have suspected it simply because I was unaware of its existence. What the two older boys – Jack and Roy – thought I've no idea, but I imagine they were as ignorant as I was, and, I suppose, as our parents were, else they would hardly have allowed us to go on this holiday. Only once did something happen that I found strange. One morning, Jack, Roy and Simon set out for a bathe, leaving me to follow them. I was in the bedroom I shared with Simon, and sitting on the bed alone, when G.E.L. knocked and called my name. On hearing my answer he entered. His expression was strained and unsmiling, and I thought he must have suddenly taken ill. He sat on the bed beside me.

'I'd like to talk to you,' he began. 'I hope you don't mind.'

There was a long pause as if he were thinking of what to say next. Then: 'I haven't had the chance of asking you if you are enjoying your holiday.'

I told him I was – very much, and there was another long pause. It struck me that he was very nervous, alone in my company. Then he said, his voice almost a whisper: 'Do you like me?'

I nodded.

'I'm very glad. I didn't know if you did!'

We sat in silence, not moving. Then, slowly and gently, he put his hand on my thigh. His grip tightened and I could feel his trembling hand. I sat still.

'You won't understand. . . but, sometimes I'm. . . very lonely. I'll never marry now. You boys are all I have.'

He stood up, crossed to the window to look out at the sea and I wondered what he was going to say next.

'I wanted to tell you that,' he said. Then he turned and embraced me and kissed me passionately on the mouth. Almost at once, he released me and left the room. Gathering up my bathing togs I walked thoughtfully to the beach to join the others.

I kept secret what had happened, for none of us had ever discussed our relationship with G.E.L. Indeed all of us were, as I now think, extraordinarily reticent about personal matters. For instance, I didn't know where the others lived and they never spoke about their families. It was regarded as 'bad form' to inquire about such things; or so we must have assumed, for I cannot remember any of us breaking this code. Games and school affairs were our chief topics of conversation. I knew that Roy, a tall pale sixth-former, was keen on history, for every morning, except on Sundays, he spent an hour making notes from Trevelyan's *History of England*. Jack, burly and brusque, and also a sixth former, was studying mathematics, and sat working at calculus.

Simon, who was about the same age as myself, never bothered to open a book because, as he boasted, he was already too far ahead of his class. In any case he thought it *infra dig* to bring along a Latin or Greek text while on holiday with G.E.L. As for myself, I'd brought *Under the Greenwood Tree,* but never found any time to read it. Sometimes we spent whole days on the beach, surf bathing; sometimes on the tennis court, playing doubles and singles; and occasionally we took trips to places like Falmouth. Once, knowing my love of cricket, G.E.L. sent me to Taunton on my own to watch a county game between Somerset and Middlesex, from which I returned exhilarated, having watched Hendren score a century.

Now, over fifty years later, that Cornwall holiday has become a faded memory; but the morning G.E.L. confessed his loneliness is still with me: also the tennis courts and the sea; the tunnels of the disused tin-mines; the little church; and, above all, the gawky figure of G.E.L. himself, walking in front with a couple of us, his face, when he turned round, smiling and happy, his wispy greying hair tossed in the wind. I suppose he was in love with all four of us, and I suppose he got nothing in return but our company. Perhaps it was enough, but I don't think it could have been. He must have desired more – much more – but didn't dare take the risk. For, after all, the consequences would have been grave. What surprises me still is how innocent all of us – including our parents – must have been. Nowadays parents would of course be much more knowledgeable and cautious. But I'm glad that our parents didn't suspect our being exposed to moral danger. As for myself, G.E.L. remains in my memory as a generous and good, if sexually unhappy, man.

After the Cornwall holiday, I saw little of him. In September, at the beginning of term, I spent two or three Saturday evenings at his home; he seemed dispirited; only Simon and I had turned up; and we both left early. After that I never went back to Bawnmore Road: I'd a feeling he really didn't want me to return and was relieved that I had dropped him. My guess – and it is only a guess – is that he was frightened that I might have mentioned at home or to the other boys something of what had happened in my bedroom at Newquay. I hadn't. The other possibility is that I'd ceased to attract him and that he needed to replace me.

I don't know whether he physically approached any of the other three, and I'm assuming he didn't. Perhaps he did with Simon, who was the youngest and best-looking of us, but perhaps not. In any event, the little group broke up, and when G.E.L. met me in the quadrangle he continued to greet me with a gruff 'Hello' and passed on. Ever afterwards I tried to avoid him either at school or at Osborne Park.

One Monday morning towards the end of the rugby season, I arrived at school and somebody told me that G.E.L. was dead. On the previous Saturday he'd been in charge of two junior matches, got thoroughly soaked with rain, and had collapsed. He never regained consciousness. When I read his obituary in the *School News* I learnt that he was forty-three years of age, which seemed to me then as old, but seems to me now as young. A few months later Simon handed me a book.

'G.E.L. left us all a book each. His sister gave me four to distribute to Roy, Jack, yourself and myself. Here's yours.'

It was a faded copy of the Everyman edition of the plays of Aristophanes.

'Will it do?' he added.

I told him it would, but for some reason I never opened it. At that time I knew nothing of Aristophanes, had no interest in Greek drama, and suspected that Simon had given me the least attractive of the books he'd been asked to hand over. Still, I was pleased to possess something from G.E.L.'s little library, though it was the wrong book at the wrong time and would not, I felt sure, have been G.E.L.'s choice for me.

Of the masters at Inst I got to know only two – Billy Greer and G.E.L. – outside the classroom, and both were repressed homo-sexuals. The difference between them was that Billy Greer seemed to find fulfilment in scouting, and happily combined scouting with teaching. Unfortunately I was never able to summon up much enthusiasm for scouting; learning semaphore, for instance, struck me as a useless exercise and I never mastered it. And the more time I spent on games and school work the less time I had for scouting. Finally I left the Inst troup. G.E.L., though he must have found some fulfilment in his teaching and in refereeing and umpiring, impressed me as a lonely and tortured man. He was given to long silences (except when on holiday), and given also (though I'd no direct experience of this) to violent outbursts of temper so that nervous boys were frightened of him and hated to be in his class. Of the two I much preferred Billy Greer for I was never able to be completely at ease with G.E.L. Besides, Billy had charm and good looks while G.E.L. lacked charm and was almost ugly. Doubtless G.E.L. with his Oxford degree in classics was by far the better scholar: I think Billy Greer had a pass degree from Queen's. But distinction in scholarship isn't of primary importance in school teaching, and Billy, because of his cheerfulness and understanding of boys, must have given dozens of his pupils a lasting love of literature and history. G.E.L. undoubtedly helped brilliant boys like Simon to gain scholarships to Oxford and Cambridge, but he must also have made dozens of boys detest Greek and Latin. So I was lucky not to be in his classes, but lucky to be one of his chosen 'pets', and for that sunny July in Cornwall I remain in his debt.

Sex played a subterranean part in the life of Inst during the years I was there. Emotional friendships between younger and older boys were common but these affairs were, I imagine, nearly all natural to adolescence. At thirteen or fourteen I experienced two emotional affairs. For some months I worshipped from afar a dark-haired pudgy boy called Savage who spent his early mornings playing handball but not, alas, with me. My role was that of a morose spectator, too shy to participate in the game. Morning after morning I rose early and cycled to school for the sole purpose of mutely admiring my favourite at play. To my fervid imagination he possessed all sorts of virtues, and my joy would have been immeasurable if he had recognised my presence and invited me to become his partner and his friend. But I'd no such good fortune: I was ignored. Not a single glance from him fell in my direction, until a year later when he sat beside me in an English class and began chatting to me. My delight turned out to be short-lived. To my dismay I became aware that Savage had a pimply complexion, a rasping voice and ugly fat knees. When he begged me to help him with his homework I discovered he was both lazy and stupid. In short, he bored me and I changed my desk to get away from him.

My second affair was equally disastrous and even more mawkish. I was attracted to a slightly younger boy appropriately enough called Kidd who, because we lived in the same direction of the city, cycled across the Albert Bridge with me. For some reason I've forgotten, I nicknamed him 'Tinkerbell' and those journeys homewards with the wind in our hair and our caps stuffed in our pockets were, for me, pure bliss. Then, after a couple of ecstatic months, these same journeys turned dull and I no longer looked forward to them. Instead girls began to attract me. The problem was of course getting to know them at close hand as it were; to explore the mystery.

There was no mystery about boys; for after rugby games we all stood naked, flipping wet towels at one another, comparing our genitals and laughing at obscene jokes which we all thought to be excruciatingly funny. I remember one pale-faced youth with an aquiline nose and a sly manner who boasted of the sexual conquests he made every Friday evening. He played centre three-quarters in the first fifteen, and when he performed poorly during the Saturday game we attributed his failure to his debilitating exertions of the evening before. But as he usually played well – else he wouldn't have retained his place – we always cast doubt on his tales. 'Oh well, you needn't believe me,' he would remark, with a wink and sly look. 'But if I didn't go out with women on a Friday night I'd play like an international. Instead I turn up like a wet rag – no spunk in me at all.' We half-believed him, we envied him, and we implored him to keep off his wild women before any of our important Schools' Cup matches. Probably he was a virgin, but certainly he had a good imagination.

Though we all talked of 'women' we meant girls; and by 'girls' most of us meant schoolgirls from Victoria College or Methodist College; girls studying for the same exams as ourselves and playing hockey instead of rugby. Nice, respectable girls who were willing to chat and giggle with us and who would stand on the touch-line at Osborne Park on Saturdays and cheer us whenever we scored a try or a goal, lingering around after the game, in twos or threes, so that they could gang up with us and go giggling along the Malone Road. I never had much luck with these girls, possibly because my attention had to be partly on my bicycle which always seemed to get in the way. Usually as soon as we reached the Old Stranmillis Road I gave up the pursuit, said 'Cheerio' to everybody, and proceeded up the hill alone. Unfortunately none of the girls lived in the same part of town as myself, so the only way to get near them was to meet them in the gods of the Opera House. And if you were lucky and cunning you might find a place behind a girl and when the lights went down you could make her comfortable by letting her sit between your legs, and later imperceptibly manoeuvre yourself so that she lay cradled against you. Such experiences were disappointingly few and never led to much more excitement other than a stroll up and down Great Victoria Street and an ice-cream in the Continental Café; which altogether constituted a fairly daring night out. There was little chance of anything serious following on these casual encounters. Even though you were sometimes given a promise that you could see her again the next Saturday night, your girl would call over her shoulder on departing, 'Perhaps'. And with the uncertainty of that 'perhaps' you lived in hope until Saturday at last came and the longed-for face was nowhere to be seen in the crowded gallery of the Opera House.

One winter grandma Leeman's health began to deteriorate. She grew thin and weak, and finally took to her bed. Because the little back room off the kitchen was warmer than her own bedroom upstairs, a bed was made up for her in the back room. Mother could then look after her better and wouldn't have to run up and down stairs.

At first father refused to visit Carlton Street, declaring that the old woman had been his worst enemy and now she was dying he hadn't any pity for her and wouldn't pretend to have. So I visited Carlton Street in his place, though I too couldn't pretend to have much feeling for grandma.

97

Whenever I called, granda Leeman was usually sitting upright in his armchair, the portrait of Disraeli, Earl of Beaconsfield, above his head, his chipped enamel spittoon at his feet. Even in cold weather the fire would be low. One cold evening I brought him a bottle of stout.

'That'll warm you up a bit, granda.'

He accepted the bottle with a slight nod, took the pipe out of his mouth and wiped his moustache with the back of hand.

'Ay, it might. It might indeed. Thanks, boy.'

He shuffled into the scullery for a big glass and poured himself a drink, carefully and expertly. Then he sat down again and raised the glass to the level of his eyes before taking a deep gulp, opening his mouth wide. Once again he wiped his moustache with the back of his hand, blew out his cheeks and sighed.

'How is grandma?' I asked.

'Same. . . no better nor no worse. . . just houlin' her own.'

He inclined his bald head, a hint that I should go into the back room and judge for myself.

She lay on her back, her eyes closed, her thin grey hair damp with sweat, her breathing heavy. The window was shut and the air stale. Sometimes her breathing seemed to stop and she lay very still as if she'd given up the struggle for life. Then her heavy breathing would return in great waves so that her whole body trembled. I stared at her face, her skin sallow and slack in old age, her nose bulbous, her mouth open as she breathed as if grateful for gulps of air. I went back to the kitchen. Granda had now put the bottle and frothy glass underneath his chair and had his unlit pipe in his mouth.

'How is she now?'

'Sleeping.'

Then, after a long pause during which he lit his pipe with its silver ring: 'Ay, Mary's dozin' away at last. My only wish is she gits away aisy at the end. That's what she wants, an' that's what I want fur her.'

I sat on the second step of the kitchen stairs, the grainy board curved and worn, and it was as if I were still attending Mount-pottinger. Then I had enjoyed coming here, especially on summer evenings when granda would shuffle into the yard to chop sticks from the little square blocks of wood he brought out of the shipyard, and I'd gather a bundle of these sticks to make fantastic designs covering the whole yard as far as the smelly water-closet with its loose seat and its bit of newspaper hanging from the whitewashed wall.

We sat in silence and I wondered whether it would be right for me to leave him before mother came back to keep him company. But I hadn't the heart to get up from the step, so I sat on, listening to the tick-tock tick-tock of the pale lemon-faced clock on the side of the staircase, the tick-tock interrupted now and again by the squirts of spittle granda ejected into his spittoon.

Grandma died a week or so later, and father, on the evening before her death, visited Carlton Street, despite his vow never to put a foot over the doorstep while the old woman was alive. But a broken vow at such a time meant nothing. He could well afford to be magnanimous. To me he admitted being glad that the old women he hated was about to face her Maker. She'd never done him a good turn during all the years of his marriage, and he fervently believed that when the time came for her to face her Maker she'd have a lot to answer for. Father wasn't an un-charitable man by nature, but for the old woman dying in the tiny back room he would make no pretence at pity; for once grandma was dead there would be a chance of a new life for mother. Of that he was convinced. It was the old woman who had wrecked his marriage right from the beginning, though why she'd set out to do it he couldn't fathom. Father believed in good and evil and had convinced himself that granda Leeman personified evil itself. When I protested that he was exaggerating he rounded on me and told me I didn't know the half of what he'd suffered, and re-minded me of the time grandma had cut my hand with her bread knife. If that wasn't an evil deed then he didn't know what was. And when I said that maybe it had been a mistake he shook his head. 'Naw, naw, the like o' that was no mistake, believe you me. . . No mistake. She meant it!' And bitterly he summed up the old woman's entire life: 'Ever since I knowed her she'd neither in her nor on her!' And what he said was true: I'd never had a tasty

99

meal in Carlton Street, and I'd never seen grandma well dressed; her clothes had always been shabby and drab and on her head she used to wear one of granda's discarded caps. There was no pride in her, father repeated to me, and I recognised that mother too had lost her pride and more than ever was beginning to resemble her mother. Grandma's death, in father's opinion, was the last hope we had for mother's redemption.

I have little interest in genealogy but I know that grandma Leeman's maiden name was Mary Herdman, and that she was born – the daughter of a railway guard – in a cottage near Saint Matthew's chapel on the Newtownards Road. Her mother, whose maiden name was Spratt, came from a farming family in mid-Down, where their descendants still possess a farm. I've more knowledge of granda Leeman's forbears (given to me in a letter by my brother Jim a few years before his death in 1976); and because Jim wrote well I'll give his own words:

'Our great great grandfather, William Leeman, was born at Armagh Braigh, two miles from Newtownhamilton and twelve miles from the county town. He was a farmer and died at the age of a hundred and two. At the age of seventy three he was blind but became rejuvenated – cast his hair, teeth, nails and got a new supply. Incidentally his son, also called William, died at the age of seventy three, the age at which the old boy got his second lease. Son William did not follow the farming, but became a flax buyer for a mill owner called Sinnet and had the reputation of being one of the best authorities on flax in the country. He came to Belfast to follow his occupation with a flax firm, Duffins, on the Ormeau Road. Later he went to Connaught where he managed a scutch mill for three years. When he returned to Belfast he apparently fell on bad times because he worked here as a labourer. Our grand-father Leeman was nine months old when he came to the city. In Armagh Braigh his mother had a grocer's shop; she was called Ellen Conn and had a brother who went to Australia. This brother – another William – is supposed to have done well out there and wrote a letter saying that he was coming home. By this time, of course, he had made his fortune. Alas, he did not arrive in the motherland and they learned later that he was murdered while at a port of embarkation. William, our great grandfather, as I said, died at seventy three; his wife, Ellen also died at seventy three. She was two years younger and therefore died two years later than he did. Our grandfather is called after an uncle James who went to America, and from whom nothing was ever heard after. Maybe he was murdered too!

'Grandfather had an old aunt living at Armagh Braigh and she, unlike uncle James, did not travel far. She was never more than twelve miles from the house in which she was born; she took this outsize gallop once – apparently to go to the county fair! Her chief claim for getting loved by posterity is that she stuck to her own wee corner in the house, and when they were rebuilding she refused to budge. And what had they to do but build around her!'

Jim wrote this years ago when I was planning this book and anxious to have some family background. And at the time he must have been busily concerned with his own affairs because his letter opens: 'the *Irish Times* wrote a couple of days ago that they were prepared to engage me as a reporter at a salary of four pounds thirteen shillings a week, plus a bonus of either five shillings or seven shillings a week. I took them up on it and at the same time resigned from the *Whig.*' And he concludes: 'I daresay granda Leeman will dig up more details about things for you after a bottle of stout – and embroider them for you after a second bottle.'

This isn't the time and place for me to write about my younger brother; indeed I don't believe I'll ever do so, but when I think of 'goodness' he never fails to come into my mind.

I did drink that second bottle of stout with granda Leeman and learnt bits about his life. I learnt, for instance, that he'd been a 'half-timer': that he'd worked in the Owen O' Cork mill on the Beersbridge Road – not far from what was known as 'Bill's School' which he'd attended and had left as a 'full-timer' at eleven or twelve. I imagine that he was at best half literate and able to read a newspaper only with difficulty, or – what is more likely – he may not have been able to read a newspaper at all. Grandma's standard of education must have been similar. For me, their lives are almost blanks; yet but for them I wouldn't have been born,

101

which is the only reason I'm interested in them now.

I know nothing of grandma Leeman except her birthplace. I don't know what school she attended, where she worked, what she thought of her husband, what she drank and how much, and why she drank; and, most important of all, I don't know what her real relationship with my mother was. Was grandma Leeman a weak-minded characterless creature? The photograph I have doesn't suggest that. Was she just a harmless ignorant woman who took an odd drink, was friendly with her only daughter, and bullied her easy-come, easy-go husband? Maybe so. Or was she an evil-minded harridan; 'a bitch out of hell', as father bitterly called her? I prefer not to think of her as that, even though father went to his grave believing that to be the truth.

But whatever the truth of this relationship, it was too complicated for father and too complicated for me as well. Absorbed in school activities which were taking more and more of my time and energy, I tried to avoid having to discuss with father the problem of how mother might be 'cured' of her alcoholism. The trouble was that mother would do well for months and father would be happy; then one day she would appear to be ill and father would at once – rightly or wrongly – accuse her of being drunk, and a row would follow. Because I couldn't understand the reasons for mother's drinking, I tried to shift part of the blame on to father, accusing him of being too short-tempered and too suspicious; while he in turn accused me of giving him no help or sympathy and of being concerned only with myself. Then, after an acrimonious argument, both of us would become sullen and resentful, refusing to speak. At meal-times the three of us would sit in silence. Finally, father would be unable to endure the atmosphere any longer, and he would thump the table and shout: 'What can be done, tell me? I can do no more! It's hopeless, hopeless!'

Driven to despair, he would threaten to leave mother if she didn't keep sober or to throw her out of the house. She had pawned his Sunday suit, her own clothes, even her wedding ring. That she'd pawned her ring and deceived him by replacing it with a valueless one from Woolworths had broken his spirit. And this deception symbolised for him that their marriage had finally collapsed.

102

One evening when I was alone in the house, reading as usual, I heard a noise at the back door. It was mother. She stood on the step, one hand on the wall to prevent herself from falling. I caught hold of her by the arm and struck her. Then I let her go and she fell on the cement path. I picked her up and carried her into the kitchen and laid her on the sofa. For a moment I thought I'd killed her, but she opened her eyes and put her hands to her head. When she withdrew them she stared at me, her eyes glazed and her face smudged with dirt.

'What happened, son?' she said, staring at the blood. And I burst into tears, terrified and ashamed.

Your acts of shame live the longest and your worst live until your death. That act I've lived with till now, and not confessed till now, but confession won't wash it away; for it cannot be expiated.

Alcoholism is a disease and is now treated as a disease – or not treated at all but neglected. Father may have heard that alcoholism was a disease. He must have, for I remember we had long discussions in which he tried to persuade mother to go into hospital; but always in vain. She shook her head and refused to go. Father pleaded with her, and asked me to plead with her, but all to no avail. Mother denied that she needed treatment in a hospital, denied father's accusation that she was a drunkard, and maintained that she was the victim of untruths. Mother, for some reason, avoided using the word 'lies', probably because she had to tell so many.

Father was a generous and uncomplicated man who, if he hadn't married mother, would have been high-spirited and full of laughter. He'd a taste for elementary mathematics, got pleasure from trying to solve puzzles or from playing whist or draughts, and most of all from mending clocks. When things were going well at home and he saw me putting away my books he used to say: 'How about a game of draughts? D'you think you cud beat me?' I never could get the better of him, and when he lifted two or three of my 'men' and was able to declare in triumph, 'Now crown that one!' his dark brown eyes would twinkle with pleasure and he'd announce to mother, 'Hi, did ye watch me wipin' the board wi' this boyo? Who's got the real brains in this house, me or him? Answer me that!'

Mother gave him years of misery and he spent most of his married life worrying about her; yet he managed to retain affection for her. In a buoyant mood he would confess: 'She's her own worst enemy, boy. . . No doubt about it. . . Her own worst enemy. More's the pity.' Then, seeking guidance, or more likely, consolation from me, he'd ask: 'What wud ye do if ye were in my place? Tell me that now.' But as I couldn't give him a good answer, he'd offer me his own advice: 'Never you git married! But if you iver do, have a good luk at the girl's mother because that's what she'll turn into at the end.'

All I know with absolute certainty is that mother recklessly threw away her life, and died prematurely because of her recklessness. Like myself, she was easily bored and found the life she was born into almost intolerably boring. Restless, volatile, gregarious, she loved gaiety and gossip and was entirely without malice. Her neighbours in Chatsworth Street, whenever they met father on his own, would shake their heads in sorrow. 'Ach Bob dear, now don't be too hard on her. Everybody has their own weaknesses, haven't they? Your Jenny'd go miles out of her way to do anybody a good turn – even a stranger. The sorry thing is she'd niver do a good turn till herself.'

CHAPTER TEN

My unhappiness at home was more than balanced by my happiness at school. After my first three years of failure to adapt myself at Inst, the following three years in the senior school brought me the success I longed for. Everything went right. The reference library was ideal for private study or for browsing through old volumes of *Punch,* and I was on good terms with my teachers – especially with Johnny Pyper and Archie Douglas.

Johnny Pyper spoke with a harsh Ulster accent, was a disciplinarian, and never allowed his class to relax. We all liked and respected him but somehow he failed to inspire us with a love of literature, probably because his voice resembled a bad-tempered dog's growl. When I was in the upper sixth I once quizzed him about the novels of D.H. Lawrence, but he cleared his throat, shook his head, and told me they wouldn't endure. I thought I knew better but didn't dare say so. If I had dared to contradict him, Johnny would have stared at me through his old-fashioned steel spectacles and given me a hearty grunt of disapproval intended to wither me on the spot. All the same, despite his gruffness his devotion to work impressed me.

Archie Douglas, a rotund Scot, impressed me even more, although he was the most self-indulgent of teachers. He was a good amateur actor, had a love of Scottish ballads and rugby, and wandered in and out of his classroom at his pleasure. He'd little method in his teaching and even less interest in the exam text books; instead, he'd read out an item of news from the *Daily Express* at the beginning of a history lesson, then inquire about a recent rugby game, then construe a verse of Horace for someone having trouble with Latin, and finally, when the forty minute period was almost up, suddenly remark in his Scottish brogue: 'Better set you your homework for next week.' But our homework was seldom done and seldom marked, and altogether I grew accustomed to slacking.

The upshot was that I concentrated more on games, playing for the first fifteen at rugby and captaining the first eleven at cricket. In addition I became a prefect and head of Pirrie House. Confident of myself at last, I was determined to get to university. Life at Inst suited me and the world outside seemed far from attractive. My own world was confined to books, games, societies and plays. Life at Inst had turned out ideal for me, but I knew it couldn't last for ever.

The cleverest and most industrious boys were entered for scholarships to Oxford, Cambridge and Trinity College Dublin. My aim was lower than that; and, in any case, I wasn't regarded as being particularly clever or industrious; so my ambition was to obtain a scholarship to Queen's and to study there for a Bachelor of Arts degree. I failed a city scholarship (which I'd hoped for) and was awarded a Hyndman scholarship which was confined to pupils of Inst. So I just managed to scrape into the university and was fortunate to do so. Conditions for study at home were difficult, and at school I spent most of my time on games and private reading. Anyway I've never taken kindly to a programme of study imposed by authority; and though I was adept enough at passing exams I never became an outstanding examinee.

When I announced at home that I'd been awarded a university scholarship the news was taken calmly, mother saying that she'd have been greatly surprised if I'd failed, and father assuring me that he was willing and eager to support me as long as he'd his health and strength and, of course, his job in the railway.

'It's not likely you'll lose your job, is it?' mother blithely remarked.

'If you tuk the trouble to read the 'Tele' you'd see for yerself the railway receipts droppin' month by month. No job's sure these days, especially a railway job. The future is all with the buses.'

'You're always a Jeremiah,' mother retorted. 'Why can't you look on the bright side of things?'

And of course father had a good answer to that.

Throughout the six years I spent at Inst father gave me his full support, though what my education would finally lead to he'd no notion and didn't care to contemplate. He left it to me to determine my own future – for how could he, an ignorant working man (as he described himself) give me any worthwhile advice? He was well out of his depth, he told me more than once, adding that he hoped I wouldn't get out of mine. But I could give him no assurance of that. All I could assure him was that I'd learnt a great deal at Inst and hoped I might learn a lot more at Queen's; but where I'd land up, at the age of twenty-two, I just didn't know. That perplexed father most of all.

My nineteenth summer was spent mostly in my hammock in the back garden, reading and supposedly preparing myself for the university. Whenever father came home from work, his face grimy, his dungarees dirty, and spotted me there, my eyes closed and my book thrown on the grass, he'd greet me contemptuously:

'So that's what you call workin', eh? Luks t'me like real hard work!'

'I'm trying to study.'

'You luk to me like the picture o' laziness.' Which was exactly what I was, lying in the sunshine half asleep, idling away my time, waiting for October and the beginning of the university term. I was looking forward to meeting girls at Queen's at something called a 'freshers' dance', and seeing them at lectures during the day and at societies in the evenings. University would be different from Inst, and I wondered whether I'd enjoy it as much. The only drawback to Inst had been that it was a closed world – not as closed as an English public school or a Catholic seminary; for by now I'd read Joyce's *A Portrait of the Artist as a Young Man* which had made me glad that my own education had been a Protestant one and that I'd never been subjected to the horrors of hell and the devil.

In the meantime there was the girl next door, a fugitive figure I occasionally caught sight of in her own garden, but who never dared to return my looks, no matter how long I stared in her direction. I liked to imagine that some day she'd respond to my encouragement; for as soon as she appeared and began weeding the flower-bed at the back of her garden, I'd vacate my hammock and pretend to examine our few straggly flowers along the border of our own garden, lifting my head from time to time to glance at her, hoping that she might reciprocate. But no return glance came, and I lacked the courage to speak to her. So my interest faded; and when I noticed her in the garden I stayed curled up in my hammock, intent on my book but at the same time never totally unaware of her presence.

Another obstacle to the acquaintance was that her parents didn't speak to mine, but went in and out with averted faces as if to discourage even the conventional greetings of 'good day' or 'good night'. Out of curiosity I used to put my ear to the wall dividing the houses when I heard sudden snatches of conversation. But my curiosity would go unrewarded, for all I ever heard were sharp cries of, 'Don't do that!' or 'Stop that!' in a man's gruff angry voice, followed by silence. Then there were mutterings which I couldn't understand. But on one occasion I heard a girl's scream, followed by a shout of, 'No! No! No!' in a crescendo of anguish. When I next saw the girl – whose Christian name I never learnt – she looked intense and sad, as if some profound grief overwhelmed her. Years later I learnt that the girl's mother had been in the process of losing her reason and had had to be sent to a mental institution. And I also learnt – from the same source – that the girl had confessed to being in love with me, but had been too afraid to glance at me lest she should meet with her father's disapproval.

Sometimes, while lying in the garden, I'd be driven indoors by a sudden shower of rain, and after bundling together my hammock to keep it dry and storing it in our outhouse where the mangle and the bicycles were kept, I'd take refuge in my bedroom overlooking the mineral-water factory and enviously watch the young men and girls of my own age joking and racing after one another during their breaks from transporting the heavy crates of jangling bottles across the yard. Their rough camaraderie was something I'd seldom experienced in my own adolescence; and father more than once reminded me that some young fellows of my age in the railway were already married; which indicated how unnaturally prolonged my own education had become, and how emotionally

108

backward I must be. In father's eyes I remained a schoolboy, intent on learning about life from books; and in his experience books were of little importance to ordinary working people who managed well enough without them. What perplexed him was the uncertainty of my future, and although uncle Willie and aunt Ida assured him that things would turn out for the best when I'd got a degree, father wasn't convinced by their arguments. 'It's all right them two blabbin' on about the future, but nobody knows nothin' about it – not even Willie or Ida. They're every bit as much in the dark as myself – or anybody else.'

Yet despite his misgivings he had promised me his support, and father's word was his bond: 'No matter what happens, boy, I'll back you up to the hilt,' he repeated, 'have no fear.'

So, with that promise ringing in my ears, I passed through the front gates of the university, proud that I could now call myself a student.

My pride didn't last long. From the first lecture, held in a large amphitheatre packed with rows of undergraduates – about two hundred and fifty in all – I had the feeling that the university would never suit me. The course was in English literature – one of the three courses I'd chosen, the others being modern history and French. Everything I loved about literature was missing; missing to such a degree that the hour spent in that herd-like atmosphere impressed me as a complete waste of time. Each place was numbered, and the professor began by noting the absentees. The sexes were separated: men were seated along the lower rows within the professor's scrutiny and therefore not likely to misbehave themselves; women were seated along the higher rows, the theory being that women were by nature docile and attentive, and would therefore be less likely to cause trouble during the lecture. And indeed they caused no trouble at all, dutifully taking notes, and sitting with pens poised, patiently waiting for bits of useful information. The men, more restless, stamped their feet in unison when the professor attempted a joke; but when their stamping met with a stare of disapproval they would stop, fearful of being asked for their name and number. They took few notes and most, looking bored, would glance at their watches every so often.

The professor – in his mid-thirties, pleasant looking, with a mop of wavy brown hair – performed his task competently enough: he recommended texts, he quoted his authors at inordinate length, and the hour crept past. Then he swept out of the room with a swish of his gown, his bundle of books in his arms, a slight smile – was it of relief? – on his lips. Then the herd rose, eager for freedom, the men trying to get a good look at the women, the women feigning no interest in the men, all making their way slowly down the stairs; down into the quadrangle and thinning out as they dispersed, some to the library in search of the recommended texts, some to the Union for a smoke and game of billiards, and some – myself among them – out through the back gates of the university and away.

By the end of the first year I was certain that Queen's wasn't the place I'd hoped for, that I'd made a mistake in going there, and that I ought to leave as soon as possible – preferably at once. But I attended nearly all of the lectures – for attendance was obligatory – and passed the exams, even though I was convinced that I was wasting my time and energy.

In the modern history class the professor, a tall urbane Scot, paced to and fro, armed with a long pointer and reading out his lecture at a pedestrian pace *twice*, so that we could write down his every word in our notebooks. As I'd been told that the lectures didn't change from year to year, and as the task of writing them out to dictation was tedious in the extreme, I jumped at the offer of a second-year undergraduate – a set of written lectures for half a crown. As a result I was even more bored, having to listen for an hour to the discourse delivered in a melodious sleep-inducing Scottish accent, the ornate prose obviously providing the professor himself with a great deal of satisfaction. To pass the degree exam it was enough to regurgitate these lectures, thereby qualifying yourself to teach history. Absurd of course; for this dull academic political history, full of incomprehensible treaties and diplomatic entanglements, taught in isolation from social and economic history, was useless, just as the English literature course, unrelated to its historical background, was equally useless.

As for French, the amiable bumbling Professor Savory, who later became a figure of fun in the British House of Commons for his reactionary views, amused his classes by turning up in riding breeches hidden beneath his academic gown. However, his lectures on phonetics, delivered in his remarkably resonant voice, were memorable; and, according to his own account, had made a major contribution to British victories in the first world war; for some of his students had won reputations for themselves as first-class translators in the army and navy and had consolidated the *Entente Cordiale*. So we were urged to pay attention to our phonetics and to follow the example of our predecessors, a sentiment greeted with enthusiastic stamping of feet and loud cheers and a smile of self-congratulation from our professor. In this light-hearted atmosphere we mouthed our phonetics and studied *Trois Semaines en France*.

I'd have been glad to quit the university if there had been any possibility of my getting a job. There was none. Ireland and Britain then, as now, were economically stagnant, and in Europe, the Fascist and Nazi movements had taken root in Italy and Germany. Despite the jingoistic propaganda of Professor Savory I'd not the least intention of fighting in another war to end wars: I'd read too many war novels, from Tolstoy's *War and Peace* to Remarque's *All Quiet on the Western Front*, not to detest all militarism, while the Officers' Training Corps at the university struck me as nothing but a ludicrous anachronism.

One day, walking across the quadrangle, I was hailed by a fellow undergraduate, who came up to me excitedly.

'Like to make some easy money?' he said confidentially.

'Yes, how?'

'You know there's a strike on. At the Northern Counties Railway.'

'What about it?'

'I've got a job there, with some others. Easy money. It's a chance not to be missed. Great fun. You'll enjoy it.'

'No thanks.'

'Come on. You might as well. You need the cash, don't you?'

'Yes, but –'

'Oh, come on. I'll recommend you. It'll only last a couple of weeks. You won't miss many lectures. What about it?'

'My father works on the railway.'

'Oh, I didn't know. . . Oh well, I understand.'

'You're a scab.'

Embarrassed, he walked away, having been given the impression that my father was on strike. He wasn't, because the BCDR wasn't involved in this dispute, but I saw no reason to correct his impression.

My reaction to scabbing by undergraduates was one of astonishment, but when I told uncle Willie about the incident he explained that he wasn't in the least surprised and had already heard of their intervention.

'You know, don't you, that kind of thing happened in the General Strike in 1926. You're learning about the class struggle. So you're not entirely wasting your time at the university.'

I'd never thought of that, so uncle Willie, backed by aunt Ida, went on to explain why such things took place. Their argument was simple. All people, young or old, tended to behave according to the interest of their own class, and as undergraduates belonged to the privileged section of society they looked on themselves as the natural allies of the bosses. Didn't that make commonsense? I agreed it did, but regarded it as further evidence that I was wasting my time at the university. So we'd an argument about that as well, with uncle Willie and aunt Ida ganging up against me.

'The more education you get, boy, the better you'll be equipped in the struggle for life. Isn't that right, Ida?'

And of course aunt Ida agreed. At such times my uncle and aunt turned themselves into a mutual admiration society. Any counter-argument I attempted was received with a sad shaking of heads, and smiles at my ignorance of the ways of the world.

Of course I'd more than my fair share of naivities: and in particular I'd romanticised the university, and was unable to face its reality. But as I was unable to face the reality of my own life at home – and escaped from it daily – it wasn't at all surprising that the reality of Queen's also proved too much for me so that I felt impelled to withdraw in a mood compounded of vexation and defiance.

Most things about the place irritated me – even the large library. At Inst I'd experienced the joy of discovering books on my own; at Mountpottinger I'd roamed the shelves of Templemore Avenue library; for years I'd explored the second-hand book-shops in Smithfield and built up my own little collection; but at Queen's free access to the books was denied ordinary students, a denial which I deeply resented. After the first term or so I gave up frequenting the library.

I ignored, too, the student societies mostly held in the evenings. Usually I'd a lecture at ten in the morning which finished at eleven; after that I was free until two or three in the afternoon. So, unable to afford eating out, I'd go home for something to eat, then return to Queen's for the afternoon lecture, after which I'd again walk the two miles home across the Ormeau park. Having made four journeys – with my ridiculous little academic gown bundled under my arm – I'd be in no mood to make two further journeys to Queen's – especially in winter when the park was closed early and I'd be obliged to take a roundabout way up the Ravenhill Road. As a result my social life, like my academic life, was minimal. I was isolated and lonely, with little money for travel and less for books. My first two years at the university became more and more dreary in the lecture rooms, while in the Union I failed to make friends with interests similar to my own. Finding university life tedious, I. went outside for intellectual stimulation.

I was lucky: a chance encounter brought me the friendship of Bob Davidson who, like myself, lived off Ravenhill Avenue. A clerk in Cadbury's office, Bob was dissatisfied with his job, hated to contemplate his future, and by reading widely was trying to remedy the gaps left by a commercial education. With his good looks he was popular with girls; and, although an amateur foot-baller, he played for professional teams. He was the companion I needed and had failed to find at Inst or Queen's.

At first we met on Saturday mornings at Davy McLean's book-shop in Union Street, which was close to Cadbury's office; there we chatted to Davy, a softly spoken ex-shipyard worker who had managed to scrape up enough money to start a left-wing book-shop in this back street off Royal Avenue. Here we socialists bought our newspapers, pamphlets and books and got acquainted with one another. Here, too, we borrowed books from Davy's lending library, noted for having copies of *Ulysses*, *Lady Chatterley's Lover* and other banned books. To be a customer of Davy's shop was to enrol yourself in a select company who were interested in socialist thought and literature; in Marx and Engels, Connolly and O'Casey, Gorki and Zola, Wells and Shaw. So Davy McLean's 'Progressive Bookshop' was my university; and there I met people who read books only because they wanted to read them and not because they wanted to acquire a degree which would lead to a good job; indeed readers attracted to Davy's shop were more likely to lose their jobs than gain promotion as a result of their reading. I suppose a few students must have found their way to Davy's, but if so I never met them. I may have seen the poet John Hewitt there, because we both can recall Malachi Gray acting as librarian in the little back room, which was really the kitchen of the house.

Davy's on Saturday mornings for a book; the Labour Hall on Sunday evenings for a lecture; that was how our week-ends began and ended. On Saturday afternoons Bob played football and I played rugby, and on Saturday evenings we drank draught cider to fortify ourselves before selecting a dance hall to dance our quick-steps and waltzes – with more enthusiasm than skill. Sometimes we picked up girls, sometimes not. As the girls, like ourselves, went in twos, four people had to agree before a satisfactory pick-up could be arranged and this wasn't always possible. The girls usually liked to return to their homes together (out of loyalty to each other, or maybe from prudence) so our encounters were brief and terminated with the last waltz, after which the girls often contrived to elude us in the darkness outside. So Bob and I walked home together, leg-weary after the football and the dancing, too exhausted even for chat, and sometimes irritated with each other following our lack of romantic success. Bob, realising that he might have better luck on his own and possessing a good tenor voice, joined a church choir and soon picked out a girl. As she was extremely pretty I envied him and taunted him with giving up his disbelief in religion for such base ends. Wryly accepting my taunts he nevertheless ignored them and continued with his affair until he decided that prettiness wasn't enough for him: although he enjoyed singing in the choir and linking arms with his girl as he escorted her home, he discovered she simply had nothing interesting to say to him. But Bob, who gorged all his girls with Cadbury's chocolates, took nearly a year to rid himself of his chocolate-box beauty before *ennui* finally overpowered him. He then took up with a more robust girl who, if not as pretty, had plenty of chat and spirit, and, best of all, not only quoted Shakespeare but even bought books of modern poetry, which she lent to him and which he promptly passed on to me. My desire, of course, was that he'd pass over the girl as well, but Bob was as stingy with his girls as he was generous with his chocolates.

Still, he couldn't be accused of being in the least stingy about sharing his male friends such as Sam Edwards, one of his colleagues in Cadburys. Sam, who was a baritone in the choir Bob had deserted, had a passion for chamber music and lieder, and invited us to his house once a week to listen to his collection of records. We'd arrive just before eight o'clock, settle down comfortably in the small parlour and spend the next three hours enraptured by Mozart, Haydn, Beethoven, Brahms, Wolf and Debussy, with a short interval for tea and onion sandwiches prepared by Sam's mother who, having fed us and washed up the dishes, would retire to bed. Outside his music Sam had few interests, and his talk was confined to discussing different interpretations of famous string quartets and singers. Bob and I were surprised when he married; but luckily for us, he delayed this until we'd listened to and discussed all his records many times. As Davy McLean's bookshop became our university, so Sam Edwards's parlour became our college of music. And after each of Sam's carefully arranged concerts Bob and I would set out to walk home from Sydenham, too intoxicated by great music to chat about such ephemeralities as local politics or football, or even the attractions and potentialities of various girls.

Having scraped through my exams at the end of my second year and with the long summer vacation yawning ahead, I was determined to escape from Belfast and, somehow or other, set foot in

France. When somebody mentioned to me that Kelly's coal-boats sometimes made calls at French ports, I rushed to their offices beside the County Down railway station and explained that, as a student, I was anxious to visit France for educational purposes. Was it possible for me to sign on as a member of a crew? The sympathetic manager said it would be irregular but possible. The upshot was that I was signed on as a trimmer, though in fact I was to be a passenger, and would have to pay the company half a crown a day for meals. He explained that the boat might reach Rouen, or might not, according to the state of trade. If I were willing to accept the terms and take the risk it could be arranged. So I told Bob of my success and he agreed to accompany me as a fellow student. We set off for France on the Twelfth of July morning, to the sound of the marching Orangemen.

The *Aran Head* was an old tub of a collier which, when fully laden with coal, lay low in the water; but when unloaded, bobbed up and down like a cork or, as the cook said, 'as if she was tryin' to kick her own arse'; and whenever this happened I became violently sea-sick. We slept in the captain's chart-room, on a great chest containing the ship's documents – a hard bed but comfortable enough; and during the day to prove our toughness we spent an hour or so in the stokehold breaking up huge lumps of coal to be fed into the boilers by the two stokers, one a skinny Welshman who worked with grace and the minimum effort, the other a clumsy Irishman from Camlough, who sweated profusely as he tramped about.

The crew quickly sized us up as two youngsters in search of adventure who, in the meantime, eagerly swallowed tall yarns of the sea. The best story-teller was the ship's engineer, a small barrel-like man who suffered from sore feet and wore carpet slippers. Twenty years before he'd left ship in South America to help build a railway there, and with the money saved had hoped to return to Belfast to open a shop in Sandy Row. Instead, he'd squandered his savings in Buenos Aires brothels and had to go back to seafaring; and now he was too old to find a job on shore.

Our first port of call was Glasgow, where we took freight for Glasson Dock near Heysham. Here we'd our first adventure – an encounter with two English girls, both of them nurses from York-shire, who were on a walking tour. When we returned to the ship the crew wanted to know how we'd fared. We'd agreed not to boast and told them that we'd had a bathe, had got the girls' addresses, and hoped to meet them again. The *Aran Head* then called at Swansea, and ran into a gale in the English Channel on our way to Honfleur. Shaky from sea-sickness, I followed Bob down the gangway and made for the nearest café. We were at last on French soil.

We stayed in Honfleur for three days in search of adventures, but none came our way; so we took walks along country roads, were brusquely ordered from a church because we were wearing shorts, enviously watched a family festival where couples danced *en plein air*, but where strangers were unwelcome, and finally had to content ourselves with a drink of cider in a dull café just outside the town. Still we'd reached France, though without enough francs to buy ourselves a decent meal or even a French book; but Honfleur was France and we were on French soil and under French skies and breathing French air and everything was mar-vellous. Though we may have thought that life in France was not as exciting as the stories of Maupassant had led us to believe, we kept such heretical ideas to ourselves; and when the *Aran Head* steamed out of Honfleur we'd no doubt that our voyage had been worthwhile. The next port of call turned out to be Sunderland, and the sight of Sunderland proved to be too much of an anti-climax. We left the old *Aran Head*, to which we'd grown attached, shook hands with the captain and crew, and made for home.

I returned to the university to read honours English and at once immersed myself in Middle English – the textbook a German publication with the forbidding title *Mittelenglische Sprach-und Literaturproben mit etymologischem Wörterbuch zugleich für Chaucer Herausgegeben* by A. Brandl and O. Zippel. The *Vort-wort* by Alois Brandl, being in German, I couldn't decipher, but was able to guess that it meant foreword. Who Brandl and Zippel were remained a mystery and didn't concern us. Only the texts did. And for months I pored over them word by word and line by line, the thirteenth-century chronicles and romances, the sacred poetry and the fabliaux, the political and elegiac poetry, and most attractive of all, the early drama – the York mysteries and Towneley plays. I was delighted too with the freshness and simplicity of a fourteenth-century lyric:

As I stod on a day me self under a tre;
I met in a morueninge a may in a medwe,
A semlier to min sithe saw I ner non. . .

But to my dismay the lecturer, a philologist, ignored both the literature and its historical background as he'd also done the previous year, which had been devoted to the study of Anglo-Saxon. A conscientious teacher, he was so pedantic that none of us could derive the slightest pleasure from his class. Morning after morning about a dozen undergraduates gathered in a dull class-room to listen to a dull lecture, with the importance of grammar emphasised and the significance of literature ignored. A.O. Belfour – a dark-complexioned bachelor who lived in Larne, which was all we knew about him – held his classes at nine o'clock so that he could depart from the university at ten and be back in Larne before midday. I learnt later that he was reputed to be a solitary eccentric who lived remote from the university and all its activities, and remote too from life in Larne: an English academic castaway thrown up on the shore of an alien country. I've no doubt that he was an excellent scholar: but unfortunately he was an uninspiring teacher. I've no doubt he was a harmless and kind man: yet he inadvertently upset the course of my life and was responsible for my abandoning the university in my third year.

The details of the row our little class – headed by myself – had with this withdrawn scholar I can still remember well; but to regurgitate them would be every bit as tedious as the lectures he inflicted on us. Briefly, what happened was that as a consequence of a printing error in an exam paper the class quarrelled with Dr Belfour and requested that the paper be reset. When we were given no satisfaction I referred the dispute to the notice of the vice-chancellor and requested an interview. It was refused. Smarting under a sense of injustice I left the university in disgust. A stupid little fracas which embittered me for a long while and which seemed likely to wreck my academic career; but a fracas which eventually I was able to turn to my own advantage. For it brought me the backing and friendship of H.O. White.

When H.O., as he was familiarly called, heard about the dispute he tried to intervene but to no avail; so he summoned me to his flat in Upper Crescent. He was then Reader in English – one of the three teachers of literature and by far the most lively one. Normally he lectured to the honours students only, though on one memorable occasion he received an ovation after deputising for the professor and delivering a lecture to the pass students. H.O. was a tall, commanding figure with a pink benign face and a slightly crab-like manner of walking as if he resented having to proceed forwards instead of sideways. He'd a habit of humming and talking to himself when he imagined he was unobserved. He was the only Irishman in the English department and the only lecturer I'd ever spoken to outside a classroom. One afternoon after a seminar on Shelley (then my favourite poet) H.O. and I had continued discussing the English romantics as we walked across the quadrangle, and then had proceeded to discuss W.B. Yeats; our shared enthusiasm cemented our friendship.

I rang the bell at number thirteen Upper Crescent and nervously waited for H.O. to appear. He'd already written to me telling me he was anxious that I should return to the university. But my mind was made up: I was finished with the place. At least I'd be numbered in Shelley's company – Oxford had spurned him – and, significantly, I'd been engaged in writing an essay entitled 'Shelley's Prose' when the row had erupted. So I felt confident I could claim Shelley as an ally; we would be fighters on the same side of the barricades. But I suspected that H.O. might be found on the other side, or more likely he'd discover a circuitous route round the barricades – if indeed he ever noticed their existence.

'Ah, how nice to see you, my dear fellow. . . And may I lead you upstairs to my den. . . Please forgive the untidiness.'

He gave me his chilly, slightly scaly hand and I followed him upstairs to his study: book-lined, many of the volumes with faded

119

spines; the carpet worn; the table overflowing with papers and pamphlets. He gestured for me to be seated; then he dramatically raised both his hands, fingers outstretched, as if something of supreme importance had just occurred to him.

'China or Indian? Which do you prefer?'

I looked at him blankly, not knowing what he was referring to.

'My sister will bring up tea in due course. But I'd better advise her first. You take. . . China?. . . or Indian?'

'China please.'

'Good. I myself prefer China at this time of day. I'll be back in a moment. Excuse me, my dear fellow.'

Never before had I been asked my preference in tea and I was unaware of any difference between China and Indian. Mother bought our tea in quarter-pound packets and father often complained that his fireman had to empty almost half a packet into their shared teacan to make a decent drink to quench their thirst. But what kind of tea mother preferred I'd no notion, except that it would be the cheapest.

When H.O. returned he began at once to try to persuade me to complete my degree, admitting that the whole incident had been most unfortunate and adding that it would be unwise for me to be unduly influenced by it. He suggested that after I graduated perhaps we might plan some exciting post-graduate work together. What did I think of his proposals? Would I earnestly ponder over them and give him my decision in due course? In the meantime perhaps we should discuss. . . James Stephens?

'I haven't read James Stephens, sir!'

'Oh you must! That's a chink in your armour! You must remedy that at once! *The Crock of Gold* is a work of. . . of genius. . . No doubt about that. A work of genius!'

He pulled *The Crock of Gold* from a bookshelf and began reading one of his favourite passages. But my mind wasn't on Stephens's fantasy and I was glad when a soft knock came to the door.

'Come in.'

His sister had brought the tea on a tray and H.O. cleared the table of its debris to find room.

'What a mess! Most untidy! Have I left enough room for the tray, Agnes?'

He introduced me to his sister, who had recently published her popular novel *Gape Row*. Agnes Romilly White, a tall thin middle-aged woman, exchanged a few conventional words with us before leaving the room. So my first meeting with a novelist could hardly be considered as memorable; much less memorable than this meeting with H.O., who went on talking about Stephens, Yeats and Pound. Then, about an hour later, H.O. stood up; the time had come for me to leave; and I followed him downstairs into the Crescent. He raised his right hand in salutation after we'd shaken hands and I'd agreed to write and tell him of my decision. My mind was almost made up, and I acknowledged his salutation as I left him.

CHAPTER ELEVEN

We moved house from Ranelagh Street to thirty-three Loopland Road, a terrace house only a quarter of a mile away in a street between the Castlereagh and Cregagh Road. Our new house in the middle of a terrace was warm, comfortable, solidly built, and with a distinctly suburban atmosphere. Like the other Boyds we were moving up in the world, though hardly enough for anyone except ourselves to notice. Uncle Willie and aunt Ida had moved to a pebble-dashed terrace house in a cul-de-sac grandiloquently called Ravenhill Park Gardens, which was shadowed by the stand of the new rugby ground; and uncle Joe and aunt Lizzie had followed to become their neighbours. So if I visited uncle Willie and aunt Ida's house and not the other, I got into trouble from uncle Joe, who always took such slights to heart. The next time we would meet in Portallo Street he would give me the sourest of looks before remarking in his most measured tone of voice, 'I was told you visited number twenty-six last Sunday. Am I right or am I wrong?'

I would have to admit that he was right.

'Does that mean you didn't think it worth your while to call at number thirty to visit your other uncle and aunt? Now why is that I wonder? Tell me why. For I've no idea myself.'

'Oh, you ask too many questions, Joe,' aunt Lizzie would interrupt with a smile. 'You know the answers as well as I do.'

'No, Lizzie dear, I don't think I do. Isn't that why I'm asking?'

'Well don't go on asking, Joe.'

'But, Lizzie, what's the harm, tell me, in asking a civil question?'

'None. But you're only teasing.'

'Oh. Nothing's further from my mind. Aren't Willie and Ida always advising me to seek after knowledge?'

I'd sit as if on needles not knowing what to reply and embar-

122

rassed at the dilemma I was in, for uncle Joe had me cornered and I couldn't blurt out the truth: that we had nothing at all in common, so why should I seek his company? Surprisingly, at least to me, all the Boyd family held him in the highest esteem. The verdict about him was: 'Joe Moreland is straight as a die.' Now that may well have been so, and it was universally agreed that aunt Lizzie couldn't have a better husband, but to my mind Joe's conversation consisted of nothing but platitudes. When I once said as much to uncle Willie his reply astonished me: 'Well I think you don't understand Joe. I never agree with him about anything, but I do like his dry wit.' The trouble was I couldn't perceive it, dry or otherwise.

But family pressure wore me down, my prejudice was tossed aside, and I dutifully paid my respects to number thirty. Convention demanded that I didn't make fish of one and flesh of the other – one of the family sayings that made no sense to me. My simple code was that you gave your company to those you liked and who liked you: the others you ignored. Curiously enough, when I didn't bother to visit the Leemans the Boyds never kicked up a rumpus. Instead they obviously approved. The complication was that I liked aunt Lizzie who, according to father, had the sweetest nature of all his sisters. Yet I was prejudiced against her too, merely because she'd selected such a dull husband. Tolerance didn't appear to be my strong suit and clearly aunt Lizzie adored uncle Joe, an adoration he fully reciprocated. Theirs was a harmonious and happy household, though their strict puritanical way of life had no appeal for me. All my inclinations were towards hedonism, even if my kind of hedonism had to be severely restricted because of lack of money. Everything considered, I was quite content with the small amount – half a crown – that father slipped into my hand every Friday about tea time with the remark: 'Will that do you, boy?' I agreed that it would. In fact I thought it generous, for I'd very few expenses. 'What you haven't got you never miss', was a dictum of father's that struck me as true the first half a dozen times he said it; but the more I thought of it the less I became convinced of its truth. And I reached the conclusion that it was false. For instance, I never had a girl of my own whom I could make dates with, bring to the pictures or to the gods, meet on a Sunday evening for a walk in the country: all that I hadn't got and most certainly missed. It was undeniable, therefore, that sexually at least, puritanism was forced on me and only my imagination could run riot, and run riot it did so that I was guilty of all kinds of debauchery.

Sex was the great taboo subject and I never recall its ever being mentioned by my parents. Father and mother shared the same bed and when they weren't on speaking terms during the day mother once or twice hinted that at night father's behaviour was quite different.

'None of that filth!' he'd shout. 'None of that!'

I would pretend not to understand what mother was hinting at, but she knew perfectly well I did, and so did father. I've little doubt that their sexual relations were unsatisfactory to both, and possibly one of the reasons for mother's alcoholism and father's ill-health. But all that part of life was cloaked in puritanical silence.

But to return to uncle Joe. I am now fascinated by him probably because I failed to understand him then. For instance, why did he christen his only son Omar Khayyam? I expect he must have borrowed the *Rubáiyát* from aunt Ida – it was one of her favourite poems and she often quoted it in his presence – and its hedonism may have struck some deep chord in his unconscious. But perhaps this explanation is fanciful, and the likelihood is that uncle Joe completely misinterpreted the poem and settled on the name simply because he liked the sound of it.

Accompanied by aunt Lizzie and Omar, he walked to Rosetta Presbyterian Church every Sunday, rain, hail or snow, disdaining public transport. For taking a tram or bus would mean supporting unnecessary employment on the Sabbath, the day when all work should cease. Indeed uncle Joe seldom used public transport even on week-days, relying on his bike to take him to work, and on his legs for any other journeys he had to undertake. As a result he was, like aunt Lizzie, as thin as a rake. Yet neither was considered mean. They merely refused to spend money on what they believed to be luxuries. They believed in simplifying their lives. That was the way they wanted to live. And mother admitted that their lives were above reproach in every respect; but she added that they were maybe 'a bit near', which was perhaps the worst ever said about them. Anyhow, mother's ethical judgments were considered to be of little value. The Morelands flourished. Uncle Joe, a natural saver of money, spent his savings on Omar's education and he eventually became a doctor of medicine and emigrated to Birmingham. Omar's career proved that uncle Joe's philosophy of abstinence brought its own rewards and was viewed as a lesson to everybody.

If aunt Lizzie married an electrician and lived happily ever afterwards, aunt Ethel married a commercial traveller and pretended to live happily ever afterwards, though all the Boyd family knew that her life was miserable. She didn't admit to misery, of course; she always seemed to be high-spirited and never missed an opportunity of extolling the virtues of her husband. Aunt Ethel was lavish with her praise, and I was given my share of it, which prejudiced me very much in her favour. But the Boyd family was aware that aunt Ethel, in extolling her partner, was guilty of self-deceit, which was something father couldn't be accused of. He faced facts and aunt Ethel refused to face facts.

In the early years of aunt Ethel's marriage to Jimmy Gunning her social ambitions had created resentment because she'd been ill-advised enough to begin married life in a spacious house facing the Ormeau Park and on the front of the Ravenhill Road no less. None of the Boyds or the Leemans had the presumptuousness to live on a main road instead of in a back street; but Jimmy Gunning and aunt Ethel had apparently assumed that such social status was theirs by rights. Their ostentatiousness caused a good deal of head-shaking and comment, and nobody was surprised when their downfall followed in due course. Jimmy, once a popular traveller with a taste for tailor-made grey suits and jaunty velour hats, began to show signs of wear in his complexion as well as in his clothes: instead of an immaculately dressed husband full of confidence and bonhomie and with a spring in his step, Jimmy gradually turned into a shabby round-shouldered prematurely-aged boozer, always thirsting for a drink, but still doing his

125

rounds in his shiny well-brushed clothes; for aunt Ethel did her utmost to keep up his good appearance. But with time his carefully polished shoes became cracked and down-at-heel, his velour hat discoloured and frayed at the brim. Aunt Ethel somehow managed to keep herself neat and tidy, and though no longer able to afford expensive clothes, she remained the smiling wife of the gay cavalier whom she saw depart for the city every morning to charm his customers and who returned to their small side-street home every evening to relate his imaginary triumphs. But uncle Jimmy's triumphal days had passed and he shuffled round the town in search of tiny commissions given to him by old friends. I never see *Death of a Salesman* without thinking of him.

If aunt Ethel had faults I wasn't aware of them. She always reminded me of mother because both were extremely vivacious – mother on her good days when all was going well, aunt Ethel in company. But vivacity was all they had in common. Aunt Ethel was a dark beauty with a high complexion and a fine figure; mother was small and dainty until middle age thickened her figure and drink coarsened her looks. I sometimes used to think that aunt Ethel would have made an ideal mother for me, but tossed the notion aside as silly. I thought it curious, too, that aunt Ethel always had a good word for mother. To me she often remarked: 'Oh, I can tell you, Topsy, I understand your mother, every inch of her. Don't pay heed to any gossip you ever hear about her. Just mind that. For there's plenty not half as good, I can tell you that much!' I warmed to aunt Ethel when I heard her say things like that, for I liked to hear mother praised almost as much as I liked to hear praise lavished on my own character.

In the later years of her life aunt Ethel used to upbraid me for not visiting uncle Jimmy and herself; but I persuaded myself that she didn't really mean what she said. Still I did visit them from time to time out of familial duty, but on these occasions I felt all three of us to be ill at ease, each trying too hard to be cheerful and sociable.

As an old woman dying from cancer, aunt Ethel, then widowed for many years, took it into her head to fly to Australia to live with her married daughter. So the Boyd clan, led by uncle Tommy, rallied round to help pay for her flight; and, once there, she wrote reassuring letters telling us that her cancer had miraculously disappeared. It hadn't of course, but she survived for over three years, and she'd been expected to live for only three months.

Aunt Alice, the most outspoken of my three aunts, referred to herself as 'the old maid of the family', but always in a tone of defiance as if expecting someone to retort, 'And no wonder you are!' She left us in no doubt at all that she had had her chances and was a spinster by choice. The youngest of father's sisters, she shared his quick temper, outspokenness, and intense family loyalty. And when I was in short trousers and very shy she used to provoke me into retaliation by teasing me: 'Oh it's easy to tell you're a Leeman and not a Boyd. And don't try to deny it!' Well of course I did try to deny it, for I'd wit enough to know it was intended as an insult. But I didn't take offence because I divined it to be true, or partly true.

Because I disliked aunt Alice's sharpness and curiosity, I kept my mouth shut when she questioned me about things at home: 'How's your mother doing these days?' The curt answer she got was, 'All right', but that only made her purse her lips as if to say, 'I told you he was a Leeman!' For my part I felt like telling her to mind her own business but didn't dare tell her any such thing. I knew my place when visiting Portallo Street and knew I had to behave myself; grandma Boyd used to clinch matters with her throaty conclusion: 'That lad knows how to conduct himself, that's for sure.' It was as if she'd guessed my own thoughts.

I never properly appreciated aunt Alice's worth until long after mother was dead and aunt Alice herself was an old woman. Only then did I realise that her hatred of mother sprang from her love of father. 'Your father's a saint,' she once told me with all the dignity she could command; and although I guessed what was in her mind and was inclined to agree with her, I thought she might have included me in the same category. But that never seemed to occur to her. Strange, that I could sympathise with her for not having found a husband, but that she never thought of sympathising with me about anything. After all, she was aware of my problems at home though I always refused to acknowledge them.

Aunt Alice lived to be nearly ninety, and in the last two decades of her life I got to know her well. Hers had been a hard life. As a young woman she had, like her sisters, worked in a warehouse where she made a lifelong friend called Bella Hopkins, also a spinster and the closest friend she ever had; they paid visits to each other's homes week after week and year after year until Bella's death. And that friendship endured even though aunt Alice had to withdraw from the warehouse when the time came for her to nurse grandma and granda Boyd through long illnesses until their deaths – the lot of unmarried daughters in many families. But Bella and she still continued to enjoy what they called 'our night out' which was the climax of their week; usually a good tea interlarded with plenty of gossip, or, very occasionally, a real night out at a concert in the Grosvenor Hall, for they both loved choirs.

Aunt Alice's life brought other unexpected compensations. When uncle Tommy married and his wife became chronically ill and unable to look after their only child, a daughter, aunt Alice assumed the role of a second mother and brought up a sensitive child to maturity. This was the emotional fulfilment which her life had lacked and it brought her such happiness and satisfaction that in old age she became younger in spirit, all bitterness gone.

Father's brothers had a greater influence on me than his sisters had – uncle Willie most of all, backed up of course by aunt Ida. At times of crisis they could be relied upon to come to my aid; indeed at one period father suggested that I should go and live with them, for only in the quietness of their home would I be able to study properly. We discussed this suggestion for weeks, but finally decided that I should remain at home. And I believe my uncle and aunt were of the same opinion. To break up a family was regarded as the beginning of the end of a marriage, and father, though often thrown into moods of despair, at other times confessed to me that time was on our side. So my relationship with uncle Willie and aunt Ida was a kind of half-adoption: I was the child they would liked to have had. Why they had no family I never learnt. Aunt Ida's barrenness was never discussed, though occasionally it was mentioned in passing: 'Children wouldn't suit Ida's style,' aunt

Alice would affirm, 'Oh, just wouldn't suit her style at all. If she'd a family she couldn't carry on the way she does – smoking, bicycling here, there and everywhere, and talking oul' politics all the time.' Aunt Alice's acerbity was of course understandable, especially as aunt Ida habitually flaunted her freedom, highly conscious of her status as the modern woman. She had an electric fire in her sitting room, an electric oven in her kitchen and H.G. Wells's famous novel about a woman's emancipation – *Ann Veronica* – on her bookshelf.

Both Willie and Ida concerned themselves with my emancipation, and were appalled that I'd threatened to leave the university after my row there. They agreed with H.O. White that I must return to complete my degree, but in the meantime suggested that I needed a rest and a change. So they planned a holiday in Glasgow. The three of us stayed as guests of an ardent socialist and his wife who brought us on trips to Oban and Loch Lomond and Burns's birthplace, all the while discussing how society should be revolutionised. Archie, a small intense Scot, contemptuously dismissed what he called 'the dope of bourgeois culture', though he agreed with uncle Willie that I should return to the university.

'I cud do wi' a label, Wullie,' he added. 'Who cudnae?'

'The working class is starved of education,' uncle Willie declared.

'Ay indeed,' Archie said. 'You mean of socialist education, Wullie.'

An argument followed about what subjects that should include, ending with Archie urging me to study the great socialist classics.

'Get a grasp o' Marx an' you'll soon understand what this sorry scheme o' things is all aboot. Ignore Karl Marx an' you'll be an ignoramus 'til the crack o' doom!'

'Isn't that a bitty too strong, Archie dear?' his wife objected.

'Naw, not at all. . . No' strong enough.'

'How about your own Rabbie Burns?' aunt Ida asked.

'What aboot Burns? What's in your mind, Ida dear?'

'Isn't he your hero? You all worship Burns, don't you?'

'Ay, an' rightly! Burns was a man an' a genius. Marx a giant an' a genius!'

129

But aunt Ida rejected the very notion of male gigantism. She accused Archie of hyperbole and reminded him of Shelley's belief that poets were the unacknowledged legislators of the world.

When I returned home I felt restored to sanity and sufficiently refreshed to face a final year of the university. Uncle Willie and aunt Ida had done the trick for me.

I wasn't on such close terms with uncle Tommy, father's younger brother, a carpenter by trade, physically the smallest member of the family, being only a couple of inches over five feet. Uncle Tommy, like uncle Willie, was a socialist and delighted in chaffing and challenging those who weren't — especially rabid unionists. He regarded social tact as feeble acquiescence to convention, and preferred a robust argument to trite chit-chat on a Sunday afternoon, a preference which made some visitors to Portallo Street leave early and often landed uncle Tommy into trouble.

I never met a less ambitious man. He was a skilful woodworker, though he professed not to have any special aptitude for his trade.

'As a youngster you got no choice what you wanted to do. You were just told you're going into such-and-such a trade, an' you thought yourself lucky to be asked. I mean lucky compared to lots of other youngsters who'd no option but the labourin'. That's the way it was. You done what you were told an' no nonsense about it. Is it much different now? I doubt it. So, believe me, you're the lucky lad.'

I was. But for a long time I'd taken my luck for granted. Uncle Tommy himself had only two aims in life: to make sure that his daughter was given the educational opportunities he had been denied; and, equally important, to serve the working class without thought of reward. Though a lively controversialist in private he never plucked up courage to speak in public; so week in and week out, he tirelessly served his union by delivering 'sick dues' to members too ill to leave their homes to collect their benefits. In this simple selfless task he found fulfilment to practise his lifelong socialist creed; and such are the salt of the earth.

Uncle Herbie, younger than my other two uncles, hadn't been able to qualify for apprenticeship to a trade because of poor eye-

130

sight, and thought himself lucky to have a labouring job in the Sirocco works. The most handsome of the Boyd males, with his fair wavy hair and clear-cut profile, uncle Herbie was regarded as the weakling of the family and his sisters often referred to him as 'our poor Herbie'. But never of course in his presence. He wanted no pity from anybody and accepted his handicap with equanimity. He confided in me more than once: 'Some people imagine I've got a miserable oul' time of it because I can't see that well. Mebbe so, mebbe not. I miss some things but not all that much.'

'What do you miss most?' I asked him.

'Well, there's the football. But the local games isn't up to much here anyway. And I get the English first division commentaries on the wireless. First-rate, boy. I can easy imagine every move in the game.'

'And what else?'

'Well, boy, I used to be a bit of a dab at the dancing. I used to enjoy a Saturday night out with a girl. A bit of a jig, you know. Had to give that up. Bumping into other couples. Became a bit of a nuisance. But, ach, everybody has to give up the dancing sooner or later, haven't they?'

Before he went blind he and I used to take cycling runs early on Sunday mornings when there was little traffic on the roads. We proceeded just above walking pace, uncle Herbie on the inside of the road, my left hand on his right shoulder to guide him. These outings, according to the family, meant a great deal to him, and they also meant a great deal to me, for he used to bolster up my morale with predictions of my future career.

'You'll go far, boy, if you're careful and don't do anything daft!'

'What like, uncle Herbie?'

'Oh well, like getting married too soon. That's daft. Bide your time over that business whatever you do. Take a leaf out of yer oul' uncle's book. I haven't yet met the girl I'd be dyin' to spend the whole of my life wi'. She'd have to be a good 'un for me to stand her. An' she'd have to be a good 'un to stand me.' And he chuckled.

'Life's like riding a bike, isn't it? You've to learn to take it easy and not rush at things. No good puffing an' blowing all the time. . . Just take everything the way we're taking this hill. We're on a wee hill, aren't we? We must be. These pedals is getting harder to turn. Let's hop off if nothing's coming. Save our breath for the next stretch. Here goes. . . Steady me, lad, else I'll end up in a ditch.'

But the time came when uncle Herbie couldn't trust himself on his old bicycle, for he could hardly see beyond the handle-bars; consequently our explorations of the Castlereagh hills had to be given up and we saw less of each other. However, he found a companion much more suitable than myself, a cheerful intelligent woman about his own age, who began by teaching him Braille and finished by marrying him.

'I'm supposed to be the fool in the family,' he whispered to me one day. 'Mebbe I am too, but I haven't done that bad, have I? Don't you agree?'

'I do, uncle Herbie.'

'We're of the same opinion then, eh?' he added in his husky voice, hoarse from smoking too many cigarettes, his only vice. And he patted me affectionately on the shoulder.

'The oul' bicycle's lying rusting in the back now, but I've got the Braille instead. And a fine woman into the bargain. Luck has come my way in the end.'

I agreed that it had.

Granda and grandma Boyd are monolithic figures in my memory. I can still see them both sitting up straight in their kitchen chairs, hardly moving and saying little, but alert to everything. And though I was named after granda I can't remember his ever showing much interest in me. I'd no idea whether I met with his approval or not, but didn't resent this because I received plenty of attention from the others in his home. I just thought it strange that he hardly ever gave me a couple of pennies or a sixpence, and so concluded that he must be doting if such an important transaction never entered his head, for it certainly entered mine. Visiting Portallo Street seemed to me a ritual not entirely different from attending church; for I'd listen to many little bits of family

132

dogma, like short sermons, and the collection on my behalf at the end struck me as appropriate to the occasion. Granda Boyd must have thought otherwise, else he'd have contributed to the coins that I liked to feel jingling in my trouser pockets.

Years later, long after the collecting days on my behalf were over, I dared to question uncle Tommy about granda because I felt I had never got well acquainted with him. I imagine I hinted that I found granda dull, if not already in his dotage, for uncle Tommy snapped back angrily at me: 'Your granda was a great pioneer in the trade-union movement in this city! Just you remember that!' And of course I have. But that was news to me then. I'd never heard a word about politics from granda's mouth during all my visits to his house; instead, he was always listening intently to father's detailed accounts of what was happening in the railway – the mechanical idiosyncrasies of various locomotives, the vagaries of firemen, guards and station-masters and, most worrying of all, the falling monthly receipts in passengers and freight, a subject which father took very much to heart. In his view the railway was periodically on the verge of bankruptcy, though uncle Willie and uncle Tommy assured him that it would last him his day. But father frequently expressed his doubts. Granda held himself aloof from these discussions, nodding his head from time to time, his left hand cupped over his ear. Of course the obvious never occurred to me: though I knew granda Boyd had suffered from partial deafness most of his adult life and had been compelled to give up engine-driving long before the normal age of retirement, I never connected his increasing silences with his increasing deafness.

Grandma Boyd was a rectangular-shaped woman who always dressed in dark clothes and long skirts down to her ankles. She moved ponderously, and when she sat down emitted a series of wheezes caused by her bronchitis. She came from County Down and spoke with a soft country accent which must have affected the speech of my aunts and uncles during their upbringing, for none had a harsh Belfast accent. I regarded her with respect and awe, and never dared to ask her any questions. Like granda she didn't appear to have much interest in my welfare, but, as my aunts and uncles had perhaps too much, I experienced no feelings of neglect. In any case, I was a self-sufficient child and preferred chums of my own age to almost any adults. I found adults – with the exception of mother – too hard to understand; as for mother I thought I understood her too well. Grandma was too remote and unapproachable, though I noticed that she liked to laugh and never lifted her voice in anger. I've no doubt that she was mother-confessor to all her children, and many family secrets must have died with her. Unquestionably father loved her, perhaps too much, for she'd all the qualities that mother lacked. Not a week passed that he didn't visit her at least once, and if by Wednesday or Thursday he hadn't put his foot in Portallo Street mother would remind him of his omission, saying with ill-concealed sarcasm: 'What's up this week, Bob, you haven't yet paid your respects?' This question was intended to start a row, and did. At such times I could have cut out mother's tongue.

Between father's and mother's parents there had never been, as far as I remember, any traffic whatever. Indeed I'd be surprised to learn that my four grandparents ever once met together after father and mother got married. Clearly the Boyds were 'better doing' than the Leemans and had little in common with them. But these two families could be taken to represent two strands in the history of the working class in Belfast during the last one hundred years: both families came from the country into the city to find work in the mills and railway; and both adapted differently to the urban environment, the Boyds becoming aware of capitalist exploitation and the necessity for trade-unionism, the Leemans remaining ignorant of the class struggle and the struggle for the emancipation of the working class. At first I was mother's son; then father's son; then, at last, myself.

Though aunt Alice detested the Leemans, she linked up the two families by her friendship with one of mother's cousins, a fresh-faced high-spirited girl called Sarah Spratt. It always struck me as strange that it should be aunt Alice who should be the one to cross the familial divide, but how their friendship began I never learnt. Possibly they met one Friday morning at the Belfast market where

Sarah went with her mother to sell butter, eggs and chickens; possibly they met at Ballynahinch Junction, the nearest station to the Spratts' small farm at Listooder, which father and mother used to visit regularly in the early years of their marriage. At any rate, the two young women met and quickly became friends; and as aunt Alice had a deep sense of loyalty, her old friend Bella was included in this new friendship, the three spinsters making up a little society independent of family boundaries. The triple friendship lasted for some years until Sarah unexpectedly married a farm labourer, took over the Listooder farm with its thatched whitewashed cottage, and her parents left for a bigger holding called 'The Ha' a few miles away.

These two farms played a part in my childhood, for from the age of seven to eleven I spent most of my holidays with the Spratt family, first at Listooder, then at The Ha. There were three sons in the family, all older than myself, and all eager for my company as they went about their tasks of milking the cows, cleaning the byres and working in the fields. With Sarah and her mother I went all over the farm in search of hens' nests, running ahead to be the first to pick up the warm newly-laid eggs, and delighted when one or other of us discovered a new nest. If we found a banty egg it would be mine for breakfast the next morning. I was the pet of the family, the say-er and the do-er of words and deeds that kept the whole family amused. I collected haws and blackberries; I climbed trees and haystacks; and I fed ducks and hens. But I was never fond of turkeys, and very suspicious of geese; indeed I'd a grudge against geese after an encounter one day as I was walking from the Junction to The Ha. Suddenly, as I was about half way to the farm, a flock of geese flew at me, hissing, their long necks directed at my bare knees. I sprinted down the road clutching my bundle of clothes, looking behind for fear they might catch me. Luckily they gave up the chase, and by the time I arrived at The Ha I'd recovered from my terror and didn't mention the incident. But I never trusted geese afterwards and treated those at The Ha warily, even though I knew they were accustomed to my company and wouldn't harm me. Coward that I was, I never made that journey alone again, always arranging for someone to meet me at the Junction so that I wouldn't have to face the geese on my own. Later on I encountered them in my dreams, their necks grotesquely elongated as they brushed against my thighs, their hissing a menacing high-pitched sound close to my ears.

What I most disliked about farm life at The Ha was the violence: the killing of poultry and animals. Mrs Spratt, who was kind to me, would wring the neck of one of my favourite hens with a twist of her wrist, then take the dead bird across her lap and pluck its feathers with jerks of her fingers, all the while amused that I should be so upset. What upset me even more was the time I saw a pig I was fond of being stunned to death by Mr Spratt with a great blow from a mallet. The blow struck the top of its head and it collapsed at once, sprawling on the dusty gravel of the farmyard.

If my memories of The Ha are scarred by violence, my memories of the smaller Listooder farm are idyllic. I passed a lot of time in the company of my pets: an orange-coloured cat who surprised me by getting fat and producing kittens, and a lazy black and white mongrel called Monkey who passed his life in my company and looked forlornly at me when I told him I was leaving for home.

The only trouble I got into at Listooder was the day I spent clambering up and sliding down a small haystack until it disintegrated and lay about the field in clumps. This game I never repeated because Mrs Spratt scolded me for the first and last time.

Despite that scolding – remembered because of its unexpectedness – the small farm at Listooder stood for all that was peaceful and happy; each summer day stretched into eternity from the time I left the cool bedroom in the morning, long after everybody else was up, to the time at night when I was asked to leave the crowded kitchen, with Mr and Mrs Spratt sitting opposite each other across the hearth, and Sarah moving tirelessly in and out the back door, and the three Spratt boys too drowsy to listen to their father as he haltingly read aloud various bits of news from a newspaper several days out of date. After my supper of milk and a slice of soda bread I'd follow Sarah and her candle into the empty bedroom.

'Sleep tight and don't let the bugs bite,' she'd say before leaving me to the darkness and the sound of Mr Spratt's voice as he stopped and started his reading of the newspaper; and I'd be asleep before two of the Spratt boys came up to share the big bed, one on each side of me, where I'd find them in the morning moving away after repeated shouts from their father: 'Get up a that, boys! Get up a that!' And with groans and grumblings they'd put on their clothes and heavy mud-caked farm boots and stamp out of the cold bedroom into the warm kitchen with its uneven flagstoned floor; and I would snuggle into the blankets and peep out at the sunlight streaming into the room from the front garden.

At the Listooder farm I was treated as the honoured guest and allowed to do what I wanted. I always found plenty to do because all the Spratts, including the dog, competed for my company. Inside the house Mrs Spratt, wrinkled, round-shouldered and long-skirted, clattered about in a pair of men's boots attending to her domestic tasks, endlessly preparing feeds for the fowl and animals and chatting all the while to the equally busy Sarah, while I sat on a stool at the side of the great open hearth, turning the wheel of the bellows gently and waiting for the turf fire to glow and burst into flames, ready for the great black pots to be angled into it. Working the bellows; watching Sarah and her mother milking the cows; helping to feed the chickens; witnessing the miracle of churning milk into butter and being rewarded with a mug of buttermilk, the blobs of butter floating on top; watching the other miracle of the bees within the beehive and Mr Spratt, with head and hands protected, rescuing the honeycomb; running messages from farmhouse to fields; carrying a can of tea or buttermilk for Mr Spratt and the three boys: I was at everybody's beck and call and the object of their curiosity and amusement with my knowledge of the ways of the city and my ignorance of the ways of the country.

Father had a high opinion of the Spratt family and they had a high opinion of him, especially Mrs Spratt, who used to repeat to me, 'You're a lucky fella to have a father like yours,' and then, turning to Mr Spratt she'd add, 'Isn't that so?' And Mr Spratt would agree, 'Ay, ay, a real gentleman.' So I wasn't surprised when father turned to them for help when mother was 'mis-behaving' herself and he, in his own words, was at the end of his tether. Threatening a separation if mother didn't mend her ways, he arranged with the Spratts that she should retire for a month to the country, away from all the temptation of the city. The retreat to Listooder or to The Ha took place three years in succession, with mother returning home with a contented and confident air, convinced that all would be well in future. But always, after a month or two, she started tippling again and resumed her old habits. Father, thrown into despondency, looked wretched, his face and chest covered with a rash so disfiguring that he was ashamed to be seen. When he shaved, blood would appear on his lacerated cheeks and the expensive ointments he bought gave him no relief. He attended the hospital week after week but the rash refused to disappear. He tried the quack remedies advertised in the newspapers but none cured him. He blamed mother for his skin infection; he blamed me for not lending him moral support; and in despair he threatened suicide. At these times he sought help from the Spratt family and mother was persuaded to go to their farm, and father had peace, at least for the time being.

My own problem was trying to make the real world coincide with the world of my imagination. Just as mother retreated into her alcoholic haze, so I retreated into my literary haze where I discovered more excitement and colour than the everyday world offered. What demons compelled mother from her domestic round I could hardly guess at: all I knew is that sometimes I hated her and treated her harshly; only rarely did I give her sympathy; and never love.

CHAPTER TWELVE

I reluctantly returned to the university to complete my degree, with father paying the fees. If father was at the end of his tether, so was I; and for both our sakes I avoided his company almost as much as I avoided mother's. I spent hardly any time at home and a great deal at the university, where I'd to take courses in maths and economics. The course in economics I looked forward to, because I'd already met Professor H.O. Meredith at the drama society for readings of Ibsen and Strindberg. An upright tall figure with a bushy beard, he wore vivid red or green shirts and was often seen striding across the quadrangle with R.M. Henry, the professor of Latin, a stocky dapper figure with cloak and monocle. Henry had the reputation of being a republican in politics and a martinet in class; and Meredith was labelled a communist because of his coloured shirts and beard. At Inst I'd discovered his slim volume of pedestrian verse in the library; I was aware of his close friendship with E.M. Forster, for *A Room with a View* was dedicated to H.O.M., and I'd dipped into his translations of Euripides. I anticipated that his course would be lively; but, to my dismay, I found his lectures dull. He droned through his notes as if he didn't think much of them himself and was delivering them only because it was his fate to teach this subject. Throughout each lecture his mind seemed far away from the Marshallian economics he was expounding, and at the end of the hour he appeared relieved that the ordeal was over and he could return to his proper work; though what that was I doubt if he ever discovered. A product of Cambridge, he gave the impression of being out of place at Queen's and was stoically making the best of his displacement. I looked up to him of course, for he had the appearance and the aura of greatness; but he was denied greatness, and his undoubted talents were somehow dissipated. Still, along with R.M. Henry and Alexander Macbeath, the professor of logic and metaphysics, Meredith stood for liberalism in a university where conservatism was the traditional norm. All I can recall of his lectures are two trivial remarks. The first: 'I see that one or two of you aren't wearing gowns and ties on this hot afternoon, and if I'd more courage I'd leave off my own gown and tie.' Academic convention however proved to be too strong and wasn't broken, and the second remark: 'I hope you'll buy a book or two of economics after you've finished this course.' Because I was one of the students flouting academic convention, his first remark sticks in my memory; and because I was already buying books of Marxist economics in Davy McLean's shop, so does the second. And although Meredith gave me a certificate of distinction at the end of his course, I profited little from his lectures. I remember references to something called 'marginal utility' but its meaning I've long forgotten.

The maths course was chaotic and the wonder is that I scraped through it. It was university teaching at its worst, and entirely the students' fault. The lecturer – a timid thin-faced man of about thirty-five – at once became the butt of a group of rowdy undergraduates who busied themselves making paper darts, hurling them across the classroom every time he turned his back to write formulae on the blackboard; then as soon as he turned round a chorus of jeers and whistles would greet him. This baiting of a diffident scholar persisted throughout the year, so that eventually the victim took refuge in silence and contented himself by writing his formulae and making no attempt at explanation. The result was that more than half the class failed the exam. Determined to pass and frightened of the humiliation of failure, I slavishly copied the formulae and worked them out for myself later; but as I hadn't done maths for four years and had lost all interest in the subject, I must just have scraped a pass. If I'd failed I'd have left the university without a degree.

I spent four years at Queen's, and when I look back I regret the time lost but not the opportunities missed: I don't believe they were there. At least not the opportunities I wanted. Still, those years brought me the friendship of H.O. White who soon afterwards was appointed to the chair of English at Trinity College, Dublin and who in due course encouraged me to pursue post-graduate research there.

In the meanwhile, having scraped a degree, I began searching for a job; but jobs in 1935 were hard to find; and I, who already had more than my share of leisure, found that society had nothing to offer me other than more leisure – the enforced leisure of unemployment.

So what father had predicted was turning out to be true: I was jobless and looked like being jobless for a long time. All my efforts had produced what looked like being a useless degree.

'What *are* you fit for, son?' father asked time and time again.

'Teaching, I suppose. Or journalism.'

'But there's dozens o' teachers runnin' the streets.'

'That's so.'

'Then what chance have you?'

'No chance.'

'Then what'll you do wi' yourself?'

I could give him no answer to that question. Ever since I'd won a scholarship at the age of eleven until now in my early twenties, I'd been a source of bewilderment, annoyance and perhaps secret pride to father; but now I felt that if I hadn't betrayed him I had certainly failed him. Mother had also failed him, had wilfully failed and betrayed him, or so he believed, no matter how I might argue to the contrary. For now, at last, I was convinced that mother was bereft of all will-power and required all our help. But father refused to accept my pleading and accused me of deserting him. Talk was cheap. I was betraying him. I hadn't to contend with mother and I wasn't responsible for her behaviour day after day and week after week. In father's company I took mother's part; in mother's company I was unable to rise above a mood of sullen hopelessness. The only way out was to leave home and I applied for teaching jobs in England and in Berlitz schools on the continent – without success. After a while I gave up sending out applications.

It was father who put me on the track of a job, and quite by

141

chance. One morning, having driven a main-line train into the Belfast terminus, he was standing on the footplate idly watching the passengers come up the platform when one of them, a businessman he knew by sight, handed him the *News-Letter*, a newspaper father never read unless given a present of it. While waiting to take the next train out he glanced at the jobs vacant column and saw an advertisement for a temporary tutor. When he came home he handed me the carefully folded paper.

'Would that job suit you? It's only temporary but it might be worth trying for. Nothing venture, nothing win. An' it'll only cost you the price of a postage stamp, wouldn't it? Why not write an application? You're a dab hand at that.'

So, at father's insistence, I applied for the tutorship and was interviewed at an address in Waring Street. A tall, thin, well-dressed man shook hands with me, introduced himself and gravely waved me to a chair opposite his desk. He sat down facing me, my letter in his hand, and explained that his son, aged nine, was convalescing from an operation and would be unable to return to his English preparatory school for a couple of months.

'If you accept this post I'd like to make it clear that the boy must not be subjected to any strain. No homework, for instance. No cramming. Nothing like that. These are the terms of employment.'

He handed me a sheet of paper; I agreed to the terms; he thanked me; we shook hands; and I was back in the street. The transaction was over in a few minutes. Father's omen that I would get the job had come true.

As soon as father returned from work he wanted to hear my news even before he'd eased off his boots and taken off his dungarees. I told him what had happened in Waring Street.

'So you got it, boy!' he exclaimed, rubbing his hands with pleasure.

'Yes. But it's only temporary and part time. Mondays, Wednesdays and Fridays, from half past two to half past four.'

'That'll hardly kill ye, will it?'

Father laughed at the shortness of the working hours, a total of six in the week. He found it extraordinary that a six-hour job

142

should even exist, not to mention be advertised in the *News-Letter*; and when I told him that the pupil was convalescing and wasn't to be allowed to study hard, father's amazement was unbounded.

'Does that mean you've to take it aisy wi' the young fella?'

'Yes, that's so.'

'Just sit on yer behind an' talk till him?'

'More or less.'

'That won't take the sweat out a ye, will it?'

Father could hardly believe our luck.

'God, I forgot to ask ye how much they'll pay you?'

'Two pounds ten.'

'Two pounds ten! For six hours a week! Sure you haven't made a mistake? You must a got it wrong, boy!'

Mother took the news clamly; she never doubted that I'd find a teaching job, sooner or later.

'But you don't understand, Jenny! They're payin' him two pounds ten for six hours! Imagine, two pounds ten! I can't believe it!'

'That must be the rate for the position,' mother explained. 'Teaching is a profession, you know.'

'Oh, I know that! I'm ignorant but not as ignorant as you make me out!'

Father was overjoyed; for I think he'd almost despaired of my ever getting anything, even a temporary part-time job; so I'd to retrace the entire interview as if to reassure him that it actually took place.

'You tell me, the father's a stockbroker?'

'I think he is, but I'm not certain. He has something to do with the stock exchange.'

'Oh, that's where the money's made. In the stock exchange. Willie and Ida say it's just a big gamblin' place where the rich get richer. Your boss won't be short of the ready cash, that's for sure!'

It was as if I'd come into a fortune, though the remuneration for the ten weeks' tuition amounted to twenty-five pounds, and from that I'd have to deduct the rail fares – thirty in all – to and from Cultra on the Bangor line. It amused father that he might be driving the train in which I was a passenger dressed up in my best clothes, and we'd an argument over whether I should travel first, second or third class. He was strongly of the opinion that I should travel first; mother's opinion was that second would be suitable, while I could see no reason why I shouldn't travel third. Father wouldn't agree to my travelling third, especially as he could get me second-class privilege tickets which he insisted he would pay for himself. So we settled that I was to travel second. That evening father slipped me a fiver to buy a new overcoat, shirt, and pair of shoes. 'You've got to be well rigged out, son, for a job like that.' And I was.

The red-roofed house at Cultra stood in its own grounds, surrounded by trees. A maid dressed in a white apron took my coat and hat before bringing me to a room with wide windows overlooking a sloping lawn. I'd just time enough to notice a log fire burning brightly, a clutter of polished furniture, a large oval table, a couple of landscape paintings, when a woman entered, holding a small boy by the hand. She introduced herself and her son, and left us, remarking, 'I'll see you both later.' The boy looked after her as she closed the door. He stood in the middle of the room, staring into space, and I wondered if he was as nervous as I was.

'Where would you like to sit, Peter?' I asked.

'Anywhere, sir.'

It was the first time I'd ever been called 'sir' by anyone and to hear it gave me a feeling of confidence and a glow of satisfaction. I suggested sitting at the table and glancing through the school books he'd brought in.

'What's your favourite subject, Peter?'

He frowned and looked uncertain. Then, after a long pause, he said: 'History, sir. . . sometimes.'

'Battles?'

'Yes, sir.'

'Have you a set of soldiers – I mean toy soldiers?'

'Oh yes, sir.'

'If you can find them, let's fight a battle on this table? Say the Battle of Hastings, which took place in. . .?'

144

'Ten sixty-six, sir,' he answered triumphantly, and left the room in search of his toy soldiers. Our lessons had begun, and I was determined that they should be completely different from the lessons I'd endured in Mountpottinger. If a lesson bored my pupil it would be abandoned at once. So, to begin with, we fought the Battle of Hastings all over again, Peter commanding the English army and I the French invaders. It proved to be a noisy and exciting battle which started on the oval table and spread all over the room, a truce being called when a knock came to the door and the maid entered with a silver tray and afternoon tea. Peter, having asked my permission, rushed out of the room, while I recovered from the Battle of Hastings with tea and muffins. And afterwards we played at arithmetic with building blocks which I'd asked Peter to fetch from his playroom. At twenty-five past four his mother came into the room.

'Well, how did you get along?' she asked.

'I enjoyed the lessons. I hope Peter did.'

'Oh yes, he did. He's already told me he likes you. And, you know, he doesn't like every teacher. Do you, Peter?'

Having shaken hands with them both and been given my hat and overcoat by the maid, I hurried down the winding drive towards the station, thankful the ordeal was successfully over. And out of bravado I took a first-class compartment back to Belfast, and wished that father had been driving the train.

I enjoyed those thrice weekly trips to Cultra to teach my pupil a little English, history, French and Latin. Neither of us took the lessons seriously. Peter seemed to look forward to my visit, for he always answered the door immediately I rang, greeting me with his polite, 'Good afternoon, sir', and leading me to the room with the log fire, but always halting at the threshold to allow me to enter first. He was a pale delicate boy who disliked his English prep school because he hated games, and he told me that the other boys ragged him and called him 'Paddy'. He always looked forward to returning home at the end of term and dreaded having to go back to school and the English boys who made fun of his accent. To my ear Peter had a perfectly good English accent, but then I wasn't much of a judge of an accent, least of all my own.

Every Friday a sealed envelope was left on the table facing my chair, and from what I regarded as decorum I let it remain there until tea and muffins arrived; then, while Peter was tidying up his books, I'd pocket it almost as if I were a thief. Which I felt I was, the afternoons being so pleasantly spent in such luxurious surroundings, with the log fire burning and my pupil quietly leafing over his books. On my last Friday, however, I opened the envelope a few minutes before I was due to leave, read a brief letter of thanks from my employer enclosed with the usual crisp notes, and began to wonder whether Peter's mother would make an appearance before I left. She didn't. As I bade Peter and the maid good-bye I wondered whether I should give the maid a tip, and if so how much. It was a dilemma I'd never faced before, and my sense of decorum failed to guide me. So, playing safe, I did nothing. But walking down the drive for the last time I felt I'd made the wrong decision.

This two months of tutoring a stockbroker's son proved useful, making me confident that I could retain a small boy's interest and could therefore teach him; and it convinced father that my prolonged education wasn't entirely wasted, at least financially, and that I could obtain a job, even though it was part-time and temporary, without what he considered to be essential – the mysterious, all-powerful 'influence' which neither of us could command and which I, in my pride, scorned. The irony of my first job was that I'd been employed by a stockbroker and that our relationship had been rigidly impersonal: the cash-nexus appeared to be all. The human relationship had been confined to my pupil who had now returned to his friendless prep school in England. The whole experience had revealed to me the comforts of life denied to my own class. A knowledge of the workings of the stock exchange seemed to be the key to success, if not to my kind of success.

What kind of life did I really want? I'd a vague idea that I could somehow combine teaching with writing, though the only teaching available was limited to a few hours of private tutoring to boys who needed help in passing exams – 'cramming' was the perfect word for the teaching I was obliged to do. As for writing, I spent months on a novel which, in the throes of composition, I assured myself was a masterpeice, but later had to admit was so mediocre that it ought to be destroyed. Yet I hadn't the heart to destroy it simply because the act of writing had given me so much pleasure. Besides, I was convinced that it had paragraphs, if not pages, worth preserving. And for years I did preserve it, until one day I tore it up and put it in the bin.

So altogether my first year after graduation wasn't entirely wasted. I spent a good deal of my time in Bob's company, foraging round the town in pursuit of girls, he complaining that he hadn't enough time to read and educate himself, and I trying to persuade him that the education I'd been given was mostly useless. I thought of us both as audodidacts slowly raising ourselves out of the morass of life in Belfast, both of us frequently making vows to endure it no longer. He envied me my years at Inst and Queen's and the leisure I'd enjoyed; while I envied him his secure niche in Cadbury's office and the stability of his life at home with his three lively sisters, his stolid Scottish father, a foreman in the Co-operative Bakery, and his vivacious Scottish mother, always busily preparing meals for her family, and always generously inviting me to sit down at their table. Sometimes Bob and I didn't meet for a period of four or five weeks when one of us had picked up a girl and surrendered our time to her; but these affairs were fugitive and when, at the end, we questioned each other we were secretive about what had happened. The 'pick-up' was condemned as 'no good' which meant that she wasn't compliant, or condemned as 'dumb' which meant that she was intellectually beneath us. Our snobbery was an index of our lack of confidence and our predatory instinct was, I suppose, that of most young men. When I read Flaubert's *Bouvard et Pécuchet* many years later I ruefully discovered that we, when young, possessed many of the idiocies of Flaubert's two middle-aged heroes.

Above all, we despised Belfast for its political and religious obscurantism. With men out of work standing at street corners, the shipyards idle, the linen trade in decline, the city was suffering from severe economic depression. Only organised religion seemed to flourish. If we couldn't clear out for good, we could at least plan more holidays away from the place. After reading Synge we decided to explore the west of Ireland, and after reading Joyce, Paris became our goal. Our imagination, stirred by our reading, gave us no peace. In the meanwhile we spent many Saturday evenings at concerts in the Wellington Hall listening to Beethoven and Brahms, Mozart and Haydn, Schubert and Schumann; public concerts which complemented our private concerts in Sam Edwards's parlour. Without music and literature our lives of quiet desperation would have been almost unbearable, and to strengthen our stoicism we attended a WEA course on philosophy given by Professor Alexander Macbeath of Queen's – a bald severelooking Scot who delivered his lectures with clarity and precision but who failed to hold our attention. In dismay, we gave up; which was our fault more than the professor's, because as a speaker he could hardly have been bettered. Our failure was probably due to the nature of the course itself, for we were expected to bite off more from the corpus of philosophy than we could chew. So we retreated from the hard chairs in the chilly room in Bridge Street adjoining the *Whig* newspaper and relaxed in the plush seats of Du-Barry's bar near the docks, consoling ourselves that we would learn more about life there than sitting in a classroom where we hopelessly confused ourselves trying to make sense of the transcendental dialectic of Kant. We couldn't deny of course the importance of classical and modern philosophy, but reluctantly had to admit our intellectual limitations.

Much later, however, when I read Macbeath's pamphlet 'A Plea for Heretics' I learnt what this rather prim and puritanical Scottish professor stood for: the need for liberal values in the illiberal environment of Belfast. His pamphlet is now forgotten – the fate of nearly all such pamphlets – and his *magnum opus*, *Experiments in Living*, a study of comparative ethics, may well have suffered the same fate. But perhaps Macbeath himself isn't entirely forgotten: he was one of the few professors who dared to speak out on social issues when professors were expected to keep silent and mind their own business.

Not for the first time Bob and I had been much too ambitious. Anyway literature was more to our taste. So instead of the great

148

philosophers we opted for the great novelists, Tolstoy and Turgenev, Balzac and Flaubert being our European choices, with lesser talents considered not up to the mark. Thus we convinced ourselves that we possessed impeccable taste. We were a literary mutual-admiration society, and saw no point in trying to increase the membership.

There must have been other young men and women suffering from cultural isolation though we were unaware of them. The university, to us, was incredibly provincial and bourgeois: a degree-giving institution, and so we scorned it. Isolation was preferable to assimilation by such an institution, and we had before us the example of Joyce in exile from Dublin's paralysis. Our *quartier* remained Davy McLean's bookshop, the second-hand bookshops in Smithfield and the Royal Avenue library.

On the verge of the *quartier* was the Labour Hall in York Street which we attended for political lectures and debates, especially during the period of the Spanish Civil War. The most memorable evening we had there was an amateur production of *Waiting for Lefty*, the once famous propagandist play about a strike of New York taximen. This short play by Clifford Odets and the lengthy novels of Theodore Dreiser made a great impression on us, and Bob ransacked the public library for all sorts of books by American writers. But despite our absorption in literature and politics we felt asphyxiated in the city and cycled to youth hostels all over the north to breathe fresh air and look at mountains instead of mills.

It was with a desire to explore new territory that we cycled to Enniskillen one day *en route* for the west of Ireland. Like nearly all Protestants of our class we knew little of Ireland south of the border, and nothing at all of Connaught except through the plays of Synge and the stories of O'Flaherty. I don't suppose we learnt much during our tour, except that the roads weren't as good as those in the North and the people much the same as ourselves. In Galway, we saw a melodrama produced by a touring company whose leading actor claimed to have performed in the Abbey Theatre, Dublin, and in the Empire Theatre, Belfast. The title of the play was *The Green Goddess* which is all I can remember about it because I fell asleep as soon as it began; for, although it was advertised to begin at eight o'clock the curtain rose three hours late; and for a good reason, as one of the actors told us: 'We can't begin until the audience gather into the hall, and on a fine summer's night they work in the fields till the light fades.' But if I can't remember the play itself I can remember the dozens of bicycles lying promiscuously along the streets near the barn-like theatre, proof that the audience must have come from near and far to enjoy the performance.

The sight of all those bicycles carelessly thrown aside outside the building, temporarily converted into a theatre, has stuck in my memory as a kind of symbol of the lives of their owners, men and women riding into the village at the end of a long day's work in the fields in order to experience, for an hour or two, an entirely different experience from that of their harsh lives spent in remote parts of the countryside. Their bicycles were their instruments of escape from the isolation of their homes, just as our bicycles provided our escape from a different kind of isolation.

On our way through Maam Cross, and passing Lough Shindilla we saw a woman's bicycle propped outside a cottage. We stopped for a drink of water. A girl of nineteen or twenty came to the door – a dark-haired beauty with blue eyes, whom we guessed to be the owner of the bicycle. When she heard our request she invited us into the kitchen to rest for a while and to meet her mother. The two of them lived in the cottage; the father was dead and the only son was in Coventry working on road construction. As we rose to depart after half an hour's chat, during which we told them a little about ourselves, the mother asked us if we'd stay and share a meal with them, telling us that they very seldom had a chance of meeting strangers. They gave us tea, farls and boiled eggs, put a fresh white cloth on the table in our honour, and we talked to them. The girl, like ourselves, was eager to leave home and see new countries; the mother was reconciled to her lot in her cottage.

'Would you like to come to Belfast?' Bob asked the daughter.

She told him she would, for she'd heard it was, like Dublin, a great city, but she thought she would first of all like to go to Coventry to see her brother and stay with him there for a while.

Maybe she would go at the end of the summer and before the winter, for the winter nights were long. But her mother said nothing to this and we guessed she wouldn't let her daughter leave home. Then the time came for us to be on our way westwards into Connemara and we shook hands and thanked them for their kindness. We never learnt their names.

After cycling round Connaught for a fortnight, at the leisurely pace of fifty miles a day, we returned to Belfast exhilarated with what we'd seen and heard, and telling everybody we met that the trouble with Ireland was that the Northerners confined themselves to the North and the Southerners to the South.

CHAPTER THIRTEEN

Private tuition – the source of my meagre income – dried up as the economic depression continued; and my flickering hope of teaching in a state school disappeared. More and more father's gloomy prophecy of my future looked like being realised: I'd educated myself out of the working class in the fond expectation that I'd better myself and be accepted into the ranks of the middle class. But it now seemed that the ranks of the middle class were firmly closed to me, and that without a trade I'd fallen socially and economically lower than father himself; unless I could pick up a clerking job somewhere, or, better still, get myself into the public library. Now *that*, in father's opinion, would suit me down to the ground. The snag was that it was a Corporation job, and to have any chance of a Corporation job you needed 'Influence'. Father, having given my prospects a great deal of thought, reached the conclusion that he'd been right after all: 'Education's all very well, but what counts in the end isn't what you know but who you know.' This conviction had led him to join the Masons; but even the Masons – at least so it appeared – couldn't help anyone like me. If father had been a reader of nineteenth-century Russian novels he'd have rightly classified me as a 'superfluous' member of society; but as he'd never read a novel in his life he was unfamiliar with the term. Naturally I didn't enlighten him. As for mother, her faith in my eventual success remained unshaken: 'Never worry, son. And don't heed your father. Things'll turn out right in the end.' A happy-go-lucky philosophy which father contemptuously dismissed as typical of mother. 'Believe that an' you're likely to land up in the poorhouse.' Which was where mother herself would likely land up if anything ever happened to him, as he so often told her. But mother paid little attention to that kind of Jeremiah chatter.

I met with no opposition when I announced that I intended leaving home for England and needed the price of a single fare to Rugby.

'Are you after a job?'

'Yes.'

'What kind of a job?'

'In a factory called BTH. But I don't know yet what kind of a job it'll be. Nothing much, I expect. Clerking. Or even labouring. Whatever turns up, I'll take.'

'D'you know somebody in Rugby?'

'Yes, two friends of mine are there. Graduate engineers. They've invited me to share a flat with them. They're looking for a job for me in BTH and are almost sure they can get me one. So I may as well try. They've influence I think!'

'Well, if they have influence. . .'

With father the magic word clinched the matter. With influence anything was possible: without it, nothing. Besides, never venture, never win, he reminded me, repeating the tag as if he'd coined it for my benefit. Then, generous as ever, he took his worn greasy purse from his hip pocket, opened it, produced the notes and handed them over. 'If you've the necessary, boy, you can go anywhere. Money makes the mare go round.' Estimating the single fare steerage across the Irish Sea and the third-class rail to Rugby, he added a fiver so that I wouldn't have to cadge off my friends. Father hated cadgers and believed that there'd be no trouble in the world if everyone paid their way and never asked for credit. His homily, though addressed to me, was really intended for mother. So, having nothing to lose but my family chains, and maybe a job to win, I left home for Rugby. For how long I didn't know. Billy McAlpine and John Bradley, my joint hosts, had sworn to me that they'd never again return to Belfast except for a few days' holiday, for that was all they could endure of the place. As graduate engineers they were qualified for jobs anywhere in the world and were determined to go abroad as soon as possible. Belfast was a stagnant backwater and they were well rid of its stench. Didn't I agree with them? If so, well, why not join them in Rugby and take the first step to freedom? Wasn't I already

153

stagnating? If I didn't clear out at once I never would. They had a spare room in their flat. They were certain they could find me a labouring job, for labourers were always coming to and leaving their factory. They were eagerly waiting for me to arrive.

Father insisted on leaving me to the Liverpool boat, and carried my small case as far as the gangway. He didn't talk much but assured me that all would be well during my absence. At any rate he'd do his best and nobody could do more than that. When the ship left the quayside he stood watching it churn up the muddy water of the Lagan as it headed towards the lough and I couldn't avoid the guilty feeling that I'd deserted him. He waved at me and continued to wave until he became a dot on the quayside, and I'd a feeling that he'd tears in his eyes, as I had in mine.

Billy McAlpine and I had known each other slightly for a long time. He'd attended Albert Bridge Sunday School but we had been put in different classes; he'd been a form beneath me at Inst; and at Queen's, because the engineering faculty was at the College of Technology, we'd hardly ever met. Like myself he'd won scholarships; and though he was scientifically inclined he'd a love of literature and music. Small, with high square shoulders, he'd a passionate desire to improve his physique – as I had – and we'd become friends when he'd invited me to go camping at Sandend near Ballywalter during the summer. Above all we loved swimming and on a hot day would bathe from early morning till midnight. At Sandend we'd lived the simple life, with a literary examplar – Thoreau – to inspire us. I earned a few shillings by coaching a doctor's son in English and French for matriculation and Billy earned a similar sum by cementing a path round a bungalow belonging to a neighbour. In Rugby Billy's companion was John Bradley, tall and handsome, the only Catholic I'd ever met at Queen's; he'd a nonchalant manner and shared Billy's enthusiasm for reading. Both had shared the same ambition: to clear out of Belfast as soon as they'd graduated. They'd taken their first step by going to Rugby for two years training to become fully-qualified engineers.

Their flat was roomy and contained hardly any furniture other than divans, a table and a few chairs. Their most important possession was a gramophone along with a few classical records and a couple of Duke Ellington's. In the evenings we'd listen to the records and revile Belfast and regret that Rugby wasn't surrounded with hills. We made plans to visit London and Paris soon; then, in a year or so, we'd all leave Rugby – which we agreed was nearly as dull as Belfast – and each of us would go forth to fulfil his ambition; John's to work in South America; Billy's to travel to the Far East; and, as for myself, the assumption was that I'd settle down somewhere to write, though there was no evidence that I could do anything other than talk about writing. (What I find extraordinary now is that all three of us achieved more or less what we then planned to do with our lives.) In the meantime my problem was to find a job so that I could remain in Rugby. Within a week I was installed as a storeman in BTH and all was well. Except the job. The wages were two pounds ten shillings a week, the hours eight to five from Monday to Friday, and from eight to twelve on Saturday. This was satisfactory enough. What wasn't satisfactory was the boredom. From the first day I suffered from a degree of boredom that paralysed me so that I became aware of the borderland between sanity and insanity. My companion in the dank airless store room was called Joe: a tall thin stooped middle-aged man with a bad limp, who never told me his surname and never asked for mine. Old Joe – as he was called by the workers who came in to collect their screws, bolts and small parts – struck me as a mild-tempered, morose man who appeared to have made up his mind that our association wouldn't be prolonged enough for him to bother about memorising my name; so he simply shouted 'Hi!' when he required my services.

'Hi. . . Twenty OBI.'

As I couldn't understand his Midland accent and didn't know what OBI were, he just grinned and shook his head and gathered up the machine parts himself, leaving me to do nothing but watch him at his work. As there wasn't enough work for the two of us Joe regarded my presence as superfluous, but for obscure reasons beyond his comprehension, he had to endure me. Sometimes a whole hour passed without anyone calling to collect 'stores', and during that hour we would stand at the counter in silence; Joe didn't encourage idle chat with someone as incompetent as I obviously was. I once asked him how long he'd been working in the store-room and he looked at me quizzically for a long time before answering. When he decided to answer he raised both hands three times, stretching out his fingers.

'Thirty years?'

He nodded and rewarded me with his dry cackle.

'I don't imagine I'll be here that long,' I replied.

He nodded and cackled again.

Though I was doubtless the most useless storeman in the entire history of the factory, my uselessness was Joe's fault as much as my own. I was eager to learn where everything was kept in the vast metal catacomb which constituted the stores, not because the job held any interest whatsoever, but only because when I was busily occupied time passed swiftly. When I was idle it was interminable and I consulted my watch every quarter of an hour during the long-drawn-out afternoons. When not busy we were supposed to stand at the counter waiting for orders; and on one occasion when I noticed that Joe had secreted in his overalls the racing-page of a newspaper and was studying it surreptitiously from time to time, I retaliated by producing from my jacket the *Selected Poems* of Thomas Hardy to learn by heart lyrics like 'When I Set out for Lyonesse' and 'Where the Picnic was' so that the day would pass not entirely without achievement.

'You're not allowed to read in here,' Joe growled, doubtless making a distinction between studying form and studying poetry, although to my mind the two activities were closely related, both requiring concentration and imagination.

'I'll risk it. They can only sack me, can't they?'

Joe's reply was to ask me if I was a student, and when I told him that I had been he nodded as if to say he'd guessed as much. That was about the longest chat we ever had; and when I left off standing at the counter with aching feet and sat reading on the dusty window-ledge where the light was best, he refrained from further comment. After my rebellious stance the job became slightly less intolerable, but I've seldom experienced such intense pleasure as the pleasure of running from that ill-lit store-room at five o'clock, down the stairs, across the yard and through the gates into the light of the anonymous streets of Rugby, streets whose names I never bothered to memorise, probably for the same reason that Joe didn't bother to ask me my name. After all, I didn't belong to BTH or to Rugby or to the Midlands; I was an intruder and a transient; but who or what I was didn't much matter. I was Irish and therefore unpredictable, and it was Joe's fate to suffer my vagaries. As he limped round the store-room in his shabby grey jacket, picking up machine parts with his grimy claw-like fingers, I often wondered what his life had been and would have been eager for his friendship, but every attempt I made was repulsed. We were too different by temperament, age and background to have much in common. I had no idea whether he liked or disliked me, but suspected he was completely indifferent to me. As I was to him, I suppose. But indifference to someone I have to work with daily is an attitude I find almost impossible to sustain. I've to come down on one side or the other, *pro* or *contra*, and old Joe never gave me the option.

I spent most of every day incarcerated in that store room and only by sustained effort of the will was I able to endure it. When I walked through the grounds of Rugby School at the week-ends and caught glimpses of masters and boys strolling about, I told myself that that was the world I really belonged to, a world of books and private study and leisure. But I'd no ambition to teach in a school that catered for the sons of the privileged classes. Anyhow my degree was hardly good enough for such a milieu, nor was my social background. My knowledge of English education derived mostly from *Jude the Obscure* which I'd read while I was at Queen's – though it wasn't on the degree syllabus, being too radical for that distinction. Still, I had to admit to being deeply impressed by the spaciousness and quietness of Rugby School in contrast to the ugliness and horror of the factory where I'd condemned myself to work. In both, however, I would be out of place and alien – either in the service of a privileged school or in the service of a soulless factory.

After a month in Rugby I'd reached the conclusion that I

157

couldn't endure storekeeping any longer: I'd have to find another job or return home; my flight to England had been romantic escapism and I found myself too depressed in the evenings to try to write; anyway, I now thought this aim merely a fanciful notion based on a desire to create something I could call my own. So I relaxed in the evenings, reading books from the public library or chatting to Billy and John about politics and our own futures. Both of them were tired of Rugby and were anxious to find jobs in London; while I suffered more and more from homesickness and was by now convinced that, unless I found a job in a school or a library, I would be happier at home. My dilemma was resolved by a letter from a friend who taught in Newry, telling me of a temporary job for a teacher of English in his school. If I applied he would recommend me. So I did, was offered the job and left Rugby. The offer arrived just in time to give me a valid excuse for returning home.

On the Liverpool boat I was surprised to find myself sharing a cabin in steerage with Professor Meredith, who asked me what I'd been doing in England.

'I was working in a factory.'

'Manual work?'

'Yes.'

'Let me see your hands.'

I held them out for his inspection.

'Ah, they're not much hardened by manual toil.'

I explained what I'd been doing in BTH.

'Good experience,' he commented. 'British Thomson-Houston is a well-known firm.'

I agreed that it was, adding that I was glad to be leaving it. At his request I took the upper bunk and we'd nothing more to say to each other.

Newry was then, as it still is, a run-down border town between the North and South of Ireland, a casualty of partition. Its atmosphere suited me down to the ground. Living in Rugby was like living in a vacuum, with anonymous people, an anonymous factory and an anonymous countryside. Newry was an Irish town, full of all sorts of surprises, circled by hills and mountains

158

and not far from the open sea. Though I'd never before stayed there I felt at home at once. I'd already climbed in the Mournes, bathed in Carlingford Lough and cycled through the town on my way to County Armagh.

The school was small, with fewer than a hundred pupils – boys and girls from the town and from the surrounding countryside. Each class had ten or fifteen pupils at most, the boys quiet and the girls shy. I taught English throughout the school, and with each day became more and more confident. The time between the first class in the morning and the last in the afternoon passed so swiftly that I longed for each period to be stretched out so that I could get to know my pupils better. It was an ideal school for a young teacher beginning a career, and I enjoyed every moment of my classes, asking questions and encouraging answers, trying to make my lessons lively and amusing, and flattered by the attention I was being given, or, at least, imagined I was being given. For no teacher knows what boys and girls are dreaming of when they appear to be giving their undivided attention.

Not only was the school ideal; I was also living in comfort. Walter Moore, who taught French and Spanish, and who had found me the job, had brought me to Miss Leo Adams's house where he himself stayed: a mansion of faded grey stucco with a tennis court, elm and ash trees in the grounds and a view across the valley in the direction of County Armagh. I'd known Walter at Inst and at Queen's, but only slightly: he'd always appeared to me to be withdrawn and taciturn, and I expect I must have appeared the same to him. Why he'd gone out of his way to find me this job I've never discovered: an act of disinterested kindness, I suppose. But during that summer term I came to know him better and to appreciate his love of French and Spanish literature. Among his accomplishments was his ability, while still at Inst, to compose verse in Spanish, an accomplishment I admired and envied, having found the composition of verse in English to be beyond my own powers. Other boarders – 'paying guests' was the genteel phrase – included two young men employed in a bank – one a clerk, the other a cashier: and Leo, who took a maternal interest in all of us, successfully found the cashier a wife but failed to reform the clerk, who too frequently returned home drunk. Not that Leo, herself an expert maker of home-made wines, discouraged moderate drinking; she didn't; and on one memorable occasion when Bob Davidson called to visit me her brew proved stronger than he'd imagined. The drunken clerk, however, became something of a nuisance and drifted away to another town; but I think Leo regretted his departure before she had had a real chance of getting him to mend his ways by finding him a sensible young woman. Marriage, to Leo, was a convenient institution to prevent eligible young men from going to the bad; young women likewise. Tall, imperious and sentimental, she loved bridge parties, preparing good food and going to Dublin to see plays. Unfortunately I was less gregarious than I might have been. So when I was alone I either spent my time in the quietness of Ivy Lodge with books, or took walks through the streets of Newry and into the hills. On four pounds a week I was able to enjoy the kind of life I'd longed for, and I'd have been happy to settle down there for life. Or so I imagined.

Aware of my interest in drama, Leo was anxious for me to meet Denis Johnston, whom she was related to, and whose plays I admired – especially *The Moon in the Yellow River* which I'd seen performed in Belfast. She lent me the autographed books inscribed to her and said she was expecting Denis to call during the summer.

'But you never know with him,' she explained. 'He suits himself and turns up at the most unexpected times. I'm very attached to him and he loves to come here. . . At least I think he does. Of course not everybody approves of Denis. You know that, don't you?'

'No.'

'Well, it's true. . . perfectly true.'

Leo puffed at her cigarette as she settled down to discuss her cousin's character.

'It's like this,' she continued, shrugging her shoulders and drawing her hand along the length of her thigh. 'Some people are of the opinion he's a communist.'

'They are probably mixing him up with Sean O'Casey.'

160

'Oh, I don't think so. Not that it matters, does it?'

'Not in the least. I'm a great admirer of O'Casey.'

'Oh, and so am I! *The Plough and the Stars* is great, isn't it? And *Juno and the Paycock*. . . And the other one. . . What's it called now. . . it's gone out of m' head.'

'*The Shadow of a Gunman.*'

That's it. I've seen them all in the Abbey. Great plays, aren't they? Of course Denis is more with the Gate lot. . . Micheal MacLiammoir and Hilton. . . What'd you call him? Never can remember his name. . .'

'Hilton Edwards.'

'Yes. Hilton Edwards. Don't care overmuch for him. . . But very talented all the same. Englishman, isn't he? But that doesn't matter. Denis once landed on top of me that whole crew – the Gate crew I mean. . . landed the whole lot here one night after midnight I think. . . without warning. . . on their way from Belfast to Dublin. They'd been playing in the Opera House. Lucky I wasn't in my bed. Yes, landed them all in for supper and drinks. That's like Denis, you know. That's his form. . . takes an idea into his head and. . . oh, I think you'd like him if you met him.'

When I arrived back after school one day towards the end of term, a dark-haired figure was sprawled along the settee in the sitting room, his face hidden behind a copy of the *Irish Times*. He looked up as I entered the room.

'Hello. Denis Johnston. Leo's away making me a cup of tea.'

I introduced myself and we chatted until Leo came in with the tea. Denis was returning to Dublin from Belfast after a broadcast and had got off the train for a chat with Leo; he proposed catching the next train.

During tea Leo and Denis chatted about their various relatives, Leo puffing breathily at her cigarettes and Denis bursting into guffaws at her stories, brushing back an unruly lock of dark hair that kept falling over his forehead. Then after tea Leo made some excuse to leave the two of us together, her motive probably being to give me the opportunity of exchanging literary ideas with Denis. Nothing of course would have pleased me more. Here I was, alone with a dramatist whose *The Old Lady says 'No'* had

161

aroused controversy in Dublin and whose *The Moon in the Yellow River* had enjoyed a long run in London; someone who had met Yeats and Shaw and O'Casey: and I couldn't think of anything to say. What Denis felt, left in the company of a young teacher he'd never met before and wasn't interested in, I can't imagine; but I suspect he'd have preferred to continue with his *Irish Times* or listen to more family gossip from Leo. Fortunately – so I thought at the time – I'd brought into the room a recently published book on abstract art which now lay on my lap. I hoped Denis would spot it and we could begin by discussing avant-garde painting and sculpture – a subject which, as an avant-garde dramatist, he was bound to be knowledgeable about, and about which I could air my own views. Unfortunately Denis either didn't spot the book (though it was a large volume and was displayed prominently across my lap), or didn't relish a discussion on the subject. So, after a silence, I drew his attention to the book, leafing it over to display the illustrations.

'Can't get anything from them. Leave me cold. I suppose it's my own fault. You're supposed to enjoy an aesthetic experience, aren't you? I just don't feel anything. Do you?'

I was nonplussed and didn't know what I felt and have forgotten what I said. Anyhow the subject of abstract art was hastily dropped, and our cultural exchange fizzled out. The next time I met Denis – many years later – we discussed Swift's relationship with Stella, a bone of contention which he would have gnawed at for hours. When I reminded him of our first meeting he admitted to having no recollection of it.

CHAPTER FOURTEEN

At the end of the summer term I left Newry and returned home to
Belfast and to another spell of unemployment. Then the temporary job I'd held in Newry was advertised and I was short-listed
for it. But a woman with more experience and better qualific-
ations was preferred. All the same I couldn't help feeling disappointed and began to despair of ever getting a permanent
teaching job. In order to improve my chances I decided to study
for an MA thesis on the novel, from Henry James and Thomas
Hardy to D.H. Lawrence and James Joyce. My subject – 'Form
and Characterization in the Modern Novel' – was at first frowned
on as being too 'contemporary' for academic research, but was
finally accepted.

As neither the novels nor the books of criticism I needed were
available in the university library, I'd once again to fall back on
the public libraries: Royal Avenue, Shankill, Falls, Donegall Road
and of course my old haunt, Templemore. I wasn't sorry to be
away from the university building itself and was glad to have a
chance of exploring parts of the city I hardly knew. I indulged in
self-dramatisation, visualising myself as 'a poor scholar'
disdainful of the proper academic tradition, but secretly wishing
to be embraced by it. However, if my pose was silly my poverty
was genuine; for no more private tuition came my way and I
assumed I didn't qualify for the dole. So once again I depended on
father's munificence.

Some days I walked from library to library in search of the
books I required, but more often I settled down to study in an
overheated reading-room in the company of the unemployed. On
wet days the reading-room would be full of men thankful for
shelter and warmth; and when their clothes began to dry out the
room would smell of stale sweat. I didn't speak to my companions

nor did they speak to me. They either accepted me as one of themselves – out of a job and in the library for warmth and a glance at the newspapers – or they were so dispirited that they didn't notice me. All of us withdrew into our own private worlds.

Though I'd opted to go on with my own research – there seemed to be no alternative – I was more and more sceptical of its value to anyone except myself. Apparently society had no use for what I had to offer, just as it had no use for my companions. They were rejects, and there were tens of thousands of them in the city, and millions of them throughout the world. I too felt a reject. But at least I was qualifying myself academically so that one day I might find a niche in this irrational social system. So I lived and worked in hope, books my salvation. My companions had no hope and no salvation. And only a few of them bothered their heads with books; most pored over well-thumbed newspapers which, as the day wore on, became more and more tattered: even the newspapers appeared to be in mourning, all of them mutilated with long black streaks to block out the racing news. Public morality decreed that the unemployed shouldn't be encouraged to study racing form. What encouragement they had for continuing their existence I never discovered.

I've seldom been able to find a job for myself – maybe because of lack of initiative, or maybe because I've the knack of making the best of things as they are, though acutely aware that they should be changed. Being unemployed didn't disturb me as much as it might have; for my time was mostly engaged with imaginative and political literature: novels by the great writers of the twentieth century, as well as the monthly volumes of the Left Book Club which uncle Willie gave me to keep me in touch with the real world. The problems of the real world of local trade unionism were his daily concern, his idea of luxury being to concentrate his mind on world politics at week-ends. Aunt Ida, on the other hand, having been defeated as a prospective Labour councillor for Shankill became disillusioned with local politics and comforted herself at week-ends with dabbling in theosophy. After all, the transmigration of souls did offer some consolation and compensation for the injustices of this world – a philosophy

164

that uncle Willie scornfully rejected as being even more irrational than Christianity itself. He hated such airy-fairy theories about reincarnation and the existence of other worlds, and grew impatient with anyone who tried to evade the serious economic problems facing human beings every day. If only people would use commonsense and apply it to social problems this world would be a far better place: so ran his argument. Now although I'd no sympathy at all for aunt Ida's excursions into theosophy, I was antipathetic to uncle Willie's commonsense. So I reminded them of William Morris and proposed the marriage of art and socialism; and when I left their house I was grateful for the half crown slipped into my hand as a reward for my contribution to the discussion.

I'd further cause to be grateful for uncle Willie's thoughtfulness; he was responsible for getting me my next job. He told me he'd heard of a temporary teaching job at the Ministry of Labour in Alfred Street and suggested that I should inquire about it. I did, and was invited to an interview. The Ministry of Labour building, a drab red-brick factory-like structure, stood in the Markets area somewhere between the gasworks and the tall turrets of St Malachy's Chapel. Its neighbours included a hoarding with garish bill-posters and a dilapidated confectionery shop. When I arrived for my interview a group of poorly-dressed girls were standing in front of the hoarding and being hailed by other girls leaving the building; then in twos and threes they all made their way up the street, with arms linked, waving and calling to little knots of youths congregated round the shop, who were lighting cigarettes with cupped hands and shouting and waving back.

'Cissie, wait on me!'
'Comin' to the pictures?'
'Give us a feg.'
'Thon's Joey! Hi, Joey, d'you want me?'
'Who's got matches?'
'Ye know where to put it!'
'Take it in yer han'!'
Guffaws and shouts crossed the street as I climbed the stone

steps to the first floor where the Juvenile Instruction Centre had its classrooms, gymnasium, woodwork room, and principal's office. My interview was with a Captain Burkett, a middle-aged, ex-Army man with a small sandy moustache and an English accent, who gave me the impression that he was concerned more with my physical than my intellectual aptitude for the job. He spoke crisply:

'I must explain to you that this isn't an ordinary teaching post in the Centre, though the man appointed may on occasion have to take a class. The Ministry wish to try an experiment. The man appointed will be given an absolutely free hand to take little groups of our students, both girls and boys, to outside places of interest. Factories, shipyards, museums. . . That sort of thing. . . also to public parks for games. Soccer, of course. . . and possibly hockey for the girls. . . Your *curriculum vitae* includes games, doesn't it?'

'I'm fond of sport.'

'Good.'

'I'm also studying for an MA.'

'Really? And you do have experience of the classroom?'

'Yes.'

'Well, thank you for coming to see us. I understand you haven't been shown round the Centre yet?'

'Not yet.'

'I'll arrange for that immediately.'

He pressed a buzzer on his desk, shook hands, and explained that he'd other applicants to interview.

I was shown round by the vice-principal, a white-haired teacher with a pronounced Ulster accent and a jaunty air of confidence. He brought me to his own classroom where about fifty boys were bent over their desks at arithmetic. None looked up as we entered. There was complete silence.

'Hard at work, aren't they?' he said, putting his hand on a boy's shoulder. 'Enjoying yourself, aren't you?'

'Yissir.'

The boy didn't look up and went on with his task; and I noticed that chalked on the large blackboard were about thirty

166

examples of simple arithmetic – addition and subtraction, short and long division.

'Good lad,' the vice-principal said in a louder tone. Then in a still louder tone added:

'They are all good lads. I couldn't ask for better.'

Not one boy looked up: the vice-principal might as well not have spoken: all appeared to be totally absorbed in their work. Not since I'd been at school myself at Mountpottinger had I seen such a large, thoroughly disciplined class.

'Now, boys, I'm leaving you again. I'll be back soon.'

That was all. No threats of what might happen if there should be any misconduct. The vice-principal had complete confidence in his class, and in himself. He then brought me on a brief tour round the Centre before returning to his own classroom where the boys were still hard at work, with not a head lifted as we entered.

'You asked me about discipline just now,' he said, smiling. 'I didn't answer you. But there's your answer.' He indicated the class.

'If you respect them, they'll respect you. I've never had any difficulty with discipline. You've met the principal, haven't you?'

'Yes.'

'What did you make of him?'

'He was very pleasant.'

'Ay, he's English. An Army man. Not a teacher. Doesn't know the first thing about teaching. However, the work gets done. It's very easy work if you know how to do it. The best of luck to you.'

A week later I was offered the post of temporary teacher in the Juvenile Instruction Centre of the Ministry of Labour at a salary of three pounds a week. I was given a room at the top of the stairs on the first floor – normally used as a waiting-room for visitors – which contained a large table and about a dozen chairs; no typewriter or telephone; nothing but a few sheets of government-headed paper and envelopes. I was empowered to take from the classrooms twenty or so boys or girls and arrange all sorts of outings for them, the ostensible purpose being to broaden their minds and exercise their bodies, the practical purpose to reduce the numbers in the large classrooms, each of which held up to sixty adolescent boys or girls. The fact that I was to be given a free hand delighted me and I could hardly believe my luck in landing the job. I've often wondered whether my appointment was really due to 'influence', the mysterious power which father lamented was denied us, but which from pride I'd have scorned to use. Had my uncle Willie, who had dealings with the Ministry of Labour, canvassed on my behalf? I never asked him, but it was strange that he knew about the job and that I appeared to get it so easily. So I had my suspicions. But despite them I convinced myself that I was the right choice and that it was the ideal job for me. The lack of constraints – no time-table to be adhered to, no syllabus to be followed, and all the conventional teaching methods to be ignored – the prospect of such freedom exhilarated me, and I set about the job enthusiastically.

For the first couple of days I wandered in and out of the classrooms, watching the other teachers at work and talking to them about their problems. The extraordinary thing was that most didn't have any serious problems, and that the Centre (as they called it) ran so smoothly. The vice-principal and the senior teacher appeared to be over fifty years old, well-seasoned men with the ability to control large classes of boys of between sixteen to eighteen, many from the backstreets of the Falls, the Shankill, the Markets, Ballymacarett and the Crumlin Road. Both of these experienced teachers used the same technique to impose their authority: no threats, no raising of the voice and, for relaxation, an occasional joke. Both commanded obedience. I particularly admired the senior teacher, a well-built muscular man with a pleasant voice seldom raised above a whisper, who won the respect of his large classes simply by force of personality. Yet his rule wasn't one of terror: the atmosphere in his classroom was calm and serene. I discovered that the only teacher who admitted to having trouble with discipline was a young and inexperienced man who hated the Centre and was anxious to get another job. 'I can't control these louts,' he whispered to me. 'Only for the senior fella next door I'd be crucified. I'd resign next week if I hadn't him to support me. Look, he's keeping an eye on us now. And these bastards know it.' With a glass panel dividing the two rooms, the senior teacher was able to supervise the class of his young colleague by remote control.

'What's his secret?' I asked.

'Age. Experience. And he actually likes these dregs of humanity. Take my advice and keep out of here. These louts'll murder you.'

The tall gym instructor, fresh-featured, curly-haired and full of bounce, was popular with the boys and adored by the girls. He at once confessed that he envied me my job and only wished that his own classes could be taken outside the building. As soon as I entered the gym I understood why.

'Smell the stench. Stale sweat. Cut it with a knife, couldn't you? I've a gym with no proper equipment, no changing-room, no baths, no showers. Everything's done on the cheap here.'

The woodwork teacher and the two women who taught the girls domestic economy also complained about penny-pinching, so clearly the Centre was inadequately equipped for proper teaching. The aim was to keep unemployed boys and girls off the streets by herding them into barrack-like classrooms where they were taught elementary English, simple arithmetic and general knowledge (including what was called 'civics'); all had physical exercises in the gym; and there was woodwork for the boys and domestic economy for the girls. If anyone misbehaved the principal had authority to 'dock' a day's benefit – about two shillings. Whether this punishment had legal sanction or not I don't know; but if it had I can imagine nothing more cruel, for nearly all these out-of-work boys and girls were ill-clothed and ill-fed. However, I was told that this course of discipline was used only as a last resort.

I chose to visit the Central Library in Royal Avenue for my first extra-mural lesson. I gathered ten boys from various classrooms, brought them into my own room, took their names, and explained the purpose of the little group. None had been in a public library before; none had read a book since leaving school; all were eager to get out of their classrooms. As we walked through the city they questioned me.

'Are you a real teacher, sir?'

169

'Yes.'

'What are you goin' t' teach us now?'

'How to use a library.'

'What for, sir?'

'I want you to read books.'

'What kind o' books?'

'Whatever you want to read. The library has all kinds. You make your own choice. What are you interested in?'

'Aeroplanes, sir.'

'There are plenty of books on aeroplanes.'

'I like travel, sir.'

'Thousands of books on travel. What country?'

'Africa. And China.'

'Any books on women, sir?'

'Yes, plenty. You'll find them in the catalogue.'

'What's that, sir?'

'A catalogue is where you go to find the books you want. You have to look up the names of the authors or the subjects. Books on women will be under W or S – Women or Sex.'

'Honest, sir?'

'You'll have to learn to use the catalogue first of all.'

'Is that hard? Cud I do it?'

'That's the first thing I'll teach you.'

'Can we all get books on sex, sir?'

'Well. . . no. Not to begin with. This class is supposed to be a general knowledge class. So we'll try to find one book on sex, one on aeroplanes, one on Africa, one on China, and so on.'

'One on sport, sir?'

'Yes. What sport?'

'Women, sir!'

I led my ragged band of adolescents along Royal Avenue, most of them smoking and passing their butts from one to the other, to be stamped out as we reached the swinging doors of the library; then up the wide staircase to the reference room, where I demonstrated the use of the catalogue cupboards. Then we filled in our application forms. We spent about an hour in the library before I told my group that the class was now over and they were free. So the books were returned and we went our separate ways.

'Good-bye, sir.'

'Thanks, sir.'

My first extra-mural group dispersed, some making their way towards the Falls, others towards the Shankill; for, with a list of their names in my pocket, I could pick out the Catholics and the Protestants. I was glad that the Juvenile Instruction Centre had at least given both sides the chance of enjoying each another's company. Indeed that was its educational distinctiveness: thousands of out-of-work adolescents were herded into classrooms at the Centre, but their religious background was ignored, though by their names it could be guessed. The staff were Protestants – at least that was my assumption – but as there was no common-room we seldom met, except for a few minutes in the corridor. However, I don't think any of the teachers I got to know would have been guilty of religious discrimination; but whether the Ministry of Labour officials, who inhabited the offices on the ground floor, were undiscriminatory in the allocation of jobs, I had no means of knowing.

Within a couple of weeks I became the most sought-after teacher in the Centre as far as the boys and girls were concerned, simply because all were eager to be taken out of the classrooms; as for the staff I think they all envied me my extra-mural freedom. The chief handicap of the job was that, like everything else in the Centre, it was done on the cheap; all I managed to extract from the principal was the price of a leather football which lasted the whole winter, and the price of a hockey ball which lay unused in the corner of my room because none of the girls owned hockey sticks.

Once a week during the winter I organised a soccer match in the Ormeau Park, about a mile from the Centre. The players – selected from the various classes – had neither jerseys, shorts nor football boots but had to play in their own tattered clothes. Yet a game of soccer was always the favourite outing, although we'd no pavilion, no equipment, nothing but the enthusiasm of the players for the game. Fond of soccer myself, I liked refereeing on a fine winter's day with a dry pitch. Many of the games were hard and

171

exciting, all the players gave of their best, their normally pale faces flushed with the exertion. Occasionally there'd be heated arguments over a disputed foul or off-side, arguments which once or twice had to be settled in the gym with boxing gloves; but the games were clean even if the language was obscene.

With the Ormeau Park available for soccer and the Royal Avenue library for 'private reading' I could always fill in the gaps of my time-table; and nearly all the firms I wrote to agreed to show my little groups round their place of business. We visited the shipyards, factories, bakeries, baths, parks, exhibitions, gasworks, the university, everywhere in the city that I thought might be of interest. In fact few of these places were of great interest – except to myself. For I gradually reached the conclusion that to bring unemployed boys and girls to watch other people at work was a well-meaning but misconceived idea; an idea which must have originated in the unimaginative brain of a politician or civil servant. How could boys and girls of sixteen to eighteen, themselves deprived of employment, look on with pleasure at others fortunate enough to be in jobs? My little groups got from these trips little more than hospitality – sometimes a cup of tea and a couple of buns, sometimes nothing at all. And some of the largest firms proved to be the meanest.

The most generous firms were the bakeries, who gave us a good meal of sandwiches, cakes and buns, washed down with cups of tea. I brought groups of ten girls on these visits to further their interest in home cookery, and possibly it did. In any case we were always happy on leaving the bakeries, and I arranged visits to as many as possible within walking distance of the Centre.

My job as extra-mural teacher had lasted about a year when somebody important in the Ministry of Labour must have decided that I was a luxury; for I was transferred to the classroom to teach elementary English and arithmetic for six hours a day from Monday to Friday. Immediately I experienced a feeling of repulsion as if time had been rolled back and I was once more in Mountpottinger, the only difference being the absence of canes; otherwise the atmosphere was much the same: the ugly classrooms, the deadening lessons, and the strict discipline. Though I was no disciplinarian, I found I was able to keep reasonable order in my classes, perhaps because of my popularity as a football referee. But once I was confined to the classroom I began at once looking out for another job. I had had enough of the Centre, and I think the Centre had had enough of me. I don't suppose I enriched the lives of many of the boys and girls I taught, but I hope a few continued to make use of the public libraries. The chief learner that year was myself.

I learnt little from the boys and girls themselves. Their up-bringing, after all, wasn't much different from my own; indeed some of them did come from the back streets of Ballymacarett. But I had never been as badly dressed – leaky boots, thinly-worn trousers, torn shirts and ill-fitting coats; and perhaps I had been a little better fed. The girls were slightly better dressed than the boys and most of them took some pride in their appearance. On the outside, anyway. They powdered their noses and dabbed a spot of rouge on their cheeks. But after gym they stank just as the boys stank. Soap and water is supposed to be cheap, so nobody needs to be dirty. That's the theory of the comfortably off. And it happens not to be true. If you live in a backstreet kitchen house with an outside lavatory and a cold water tap in the scullery, and a towel or two for the whole family, and no privacy for a thorough wash, and no clean clothes to change into, naturally you begin to smell. And when you're herded into a classroom with fifty other boys or girls all living the same way as yourself, and the windows are closed, there is a stench. And there was always a stench in the 'Buroo School', to give it the name it was known by. Only we teachers called it the 'Centre'.

I kept out of the building as much as I could; even on wet days I brought my teams to the park to play football on a muddy pitch, knowing they preferred to get soaked rather than endure the tedium of the classroom, though there they'd be warm and com-fortable. On other wet days we'd walk to the library, select our books and read for a while in our damp clothes. Then I'd give my group their freedom.

What I liked most about this job was the opportunity it gave me to learn something of the conditions of industry. I already knew a little about the railway, having stood with father on the footplate; and uncle Herbie had shown me through the Sirocco works one Sunday when the place was deserted. What started this curiosity I don't know, for I had no idealistic notions about the dignity of labour; manual work struck me as boringly repetitive. Still, father's job had a certain fascination, and sometimes I wished he had encouraged me to follow in his and granda Boyd's footsteps. At least an engine-driver enjoyed a sense of freedom: I often heard him referring to himself as being always 'on the wing'. This wingedness – though it was noisy and dirty – made a deep appeal to me. It was a tough job, but then I thought of myself as fairly tough; which was why I enjoyed rugby. And father himself was tough, with strong hands and arms and a deep chest. Yet I'd often seen him come home exhausted after a twelve-hour shift in winter, his face raw with the wind. And he would collapse on the sofa with hardly enough energy to unlace his boots and pull off his oil-soaked grimy dungarees.

'This overtime's too much, and I'm daft to do it, boy.'

And he'd puff at his cigarette and look at me through his tired red-rimmed eyes. 'You don't understan' what it takes out of me.'

It was father who made me conscious of the indignity of labour. 'The big fellas – the managers – know nothin' an' care nothin' about our conditions. An' why should they? They think we're well paid an' have nothin' to complain about. An' they know there's plenty of others waitin' to grab our jobs.' In particular he resented the indignity of having to eat his sandwiches with filthy hands and drink his tea out of a smoky tin can. He was a fastidious man and liked to have clean shirts, well-fitted suits and good boots. Indeed he'd a sense of orderliness which I haven't inherited; if he came across untidiness in the house – which he frequently did – he'd clear it up with the remark: 'Things should be in their place', and add sententiously in a mock-clerical tone: 'There's a place for everything and everything should be in its place.' It was an injunction mother and I found impossible to follow, both of us being too careless by temperament. So my streak of suppressed bohemianism derives from mother, and any sense of order I have from father. But orderliness never comes easily to me and careless-

174

ness does; I'm both mother's and father's child.

I took advantage of my time at the Juvenile Instruction Centre by learning something of how thousands of people spend their working lives. I'd had fleeting glimpses of workers in many industries and had no wish to spend my life in such conditions. If industrialism wasn't slavery it was near enough to what I imagined slavery to be. By comparison teaching was child's play, even though the classes in the Centre were much too large. The very act of teaching gave you dignity, while the very act of being a unit on a conveyor-belt or having to work in bare feet in a 'wet' spinnng room deprived you of all dignity. The drawback with teaching was that it was a sheltered profession, and unsuitable for anyone with aspirations to be a writer.

I had of course a very romantic notion of what being a writer meant. To me then, it meant travelling to exotic places, like Robert Louis Stevenson or D.H. Lawrence; it meant having adventures, particularly amorous ones; it meant having intimate knowledge of great cities, as Dickens had of London or Balzac of Paris; it meant freedom and leisure and happiness and recognition. In the meantime I was teaching hundreds of half-starved adolescents whose futures were bleak. My own future didn't seem too bright either. Why not make a start by writing about what was happening to unemployed boys and girls?

This was easily done, and my anonymous articles appeared in the *Irish Democrat*, a socialist paper with a tiny circulation. But at least I'd begun on my secret pilgrimage. I wasn't writing for money or for esteem but because I'd something I wanted to say. I was writing because I was indignant about the miserable conditions of young workers. My model was *The Condition of the Working Class in England in 1844* by Frederick Engels, which I thought a masterpiece. It is. And Engels was twenty-four when he wrote it, the same age as I was myself.

The disadvantage of being brought up in a working-class street in Belfast was that civilisation seemed far away and inaccessible and barbarism too close and dangerous. From the beginning of my childhood violence had always been round the corner. In

Chatsworth Street we had lived too close to the rowdy pubs in Lord Street and the squalor of the Gut. I remember a drunk with close-cropped hair displaying for us children the baton scars on his skull and in a hoarse maudlin voice telling us how the police had kicked him unconscious before arresting him; and how he feared they'd arrest him again. We listened with wide eyes and open mouths to his drunken talk, for no one else paid attention to him as he lay sprawled on the pavement, until at last he cradled his head on his arm and fell asleep and we left him where he lay. At home there was always talk of the riots, but, much to my dismay, rioting nearly always broke out when I was in bed, and so I had to be satisfied with the cowboy pictures I sat watching, goggle-eyed, in the New Princess. Once there was a good riot in Templemore Avenue and a Catholic spirit grocer's shop was looted and set on fire, but when I was allowed out all I saw were the smouldering ruins.

Fight for Billy!
Fight for Billy!
Fight for the Cock o' the North!

That was one of the best songs, and we used to shout it at the top of our voices as we paraded round the smelly back entries in defiance of the Catholics who were preparing to attack us. That none of us had ever seen a Catholic or knew anything about the 'Cock o' the North' didn't matter in the least. Somewhere near us there was a big fight on and we Protestants wanted to be on the winning side.

Such was the childish militancy of my early years of barbarism: the years before the civilising influence of books blew it away. I found intellectual liberation in Davy McLean's bookshop, the public libraries, the second-hand shops at Smithfield and in Uncle Willie's book shelves. I felt I belonged to the cultural vanguard of Belfast. And at some meeting or other I had become acquainted with John Hewitt, poet and art critic, who worked in the Museum and Art Gallery at Stranmillis, and who on one occasion had lectured to my group of unemployed boys. He was the first local intellectual I'd ever met – a portly pink-cheeked figure who exuded confidence whether he was talking about poetry or politics. A few years older than myself, married to Roberta, a dark attractive woman, John was the centre of a small circle of left-wingers who thought the intellectual life of the city stagnant and who, by political action and thought, were trying to stir things up. I admired him but felt ill at ease in his company; he had read far too much for me to challenge his opinions; and many years elapsed before I found out, by quizzing Roberta, that John's apparent arrogance was a disguise covering his shyness. And shyness was one of my own afflictions. Neither at Inst nor at Queen's had I the courage to participate in the debating societies, and in the Labour Hall, when discussion after the lecture was invited, I always sat mute. In any case, the cut-and-thrust of noisy argument struck me as a waste of time and energy; so when a socialist meeting turned too emotional I felt inclined to walk out, though I lacked the courage to do even that.

Politically the Unionists retained a firm grip on the city and on the six northern counties, their slogan – one of many – 'What we have we hold.' A well organised party, backed by the Protestants of all classes – the gentry, the farmers, the employers, the professions and the industrial workers – it appeared to hold an impregnable position in the statelet it ruled. Only a small minority of Protestants refused to give the ruling party their allegiance; and dissent was interpreted as the equivalent of treason; and treason meant ostracism.

All this, however, I took for granted. I hated political conservatism in general and local unionism in particular; I had made a few friends; and as long as I had books and music I'd never fall into despondency – provided I'd some congenial work to do. And my two years at the Juvenile Instruction Centre had given me money and time to look around. From my three pounds a week I gave father two, keeping one for myself, and at the end of the year I'd saved enough for a holiday in Paris, travelling steerage and third class. George Moore and J.M. Synge had lived in Paris: James Joyce was living in Paris; Paris – not Dublin or London – was the essential city to see, explore, breathe its air, listen to its sounds, speak its language. To be in Paris was to taste and touch civilisation.

CHAPTER FIFTEEN

July is the best month to escape from Belfast because then the Orangemen are constantly on parade, the atmosphere is tense, riots occur, and people who can afford a holiday leave the city. Bob and I planned to leave before the Twelfth, when the city appears to be *en fête* for the Protestant cause. It is the most divisive day of the year, and to me the saddest.

We wanted to be in Paris for the *Quatorze* when the French nation was *en fête*; and there we could join in the procession. We travelled by the cheapest route and arrived at Gare Saint-Lazare in the very early morning, exhausted. We struggled as far as the Place de L'Opéra, spotted two empty benches and fell asleep: to be awakened by the sound of a brass band. It was a twelfth of July morning and for a moment I imagined that the Orangemen had invaded Paris. It was a French Salvation Army band on Sunday parade.

Not having booked a hotel, and without a map of Paris, we felt lost. So, hungry and drowsy, we took the first autobus that came along. Its destination was Montmartre; and that magic name, familiar from our reading of French novels, beckoned us on. We got off at Place Pigalle and found a room on the top floor of the small Hôtel de l' Epoque in the Rue Germain-Pilon, overlooking the Boulevard de Clichy.

It was a cheap hotel, our room on the top *étage*, and the traffic from the boulevard below didn't disturb us. We could see the roofs of Paris from our tiny balcony where we took our *petit déjeuner* every morning – coffee and two croissants – then smoked a French cigarette and used the ridiculously small *lavabo* which made us laugh, followed by our use of the *bidet* which made us laugh even more. We made friends with the *patronne*, Madame Landragin, a small, dark, smiling figure who also made us laugh when she tried to speak English, running in and out of her cubicle of an office to consult her little dictionary. Then she introduced us to her husband, who told us he'd been a boxer and had once fought in the Ulster Hall and had good memories of Belfast; but now, in early middle age, his boxing days were long past, and he spent his days fishing in the Seine and keeping out of his wife's way. He loved Paris and he loved his wife and he loved, above all, his fishing. Life was good, very good but he sometimes wished he was younger, and he winked. He expressed the opinion that we were exactly the right age to come to Paris for the first time, and he hoped it would be the first of many times. Then he offered us a Gitane and Madame gave us a glass of red wine and we chattered till Madame's face grew serious. Her expression indicated that she'd spent enough of her time with us, and she glanced at her husband, who was more prodigal with his time and more loquacious, but at last he gave way to her, after having displayed his male dominance. So we shook hands, and went out into the hubbub of the boulevard.

In the afternoons and at night two or three *putains* loitered about the hallway, now and then darting across the narrow St Germain-Pilon in search of a client, swinging their hips and their shiny black handbags. Sometimes we met one of them leading a man upstairs into a bedroom. Our little hotel, if not a brothel, served the trade. We assumed that all the other little hotels did the same, for business was business. But timidity as well as squeamishness prevented us from accepting the services of the local *putains*, who ceased to accost us after a few polite rebuffs of '*Pas ce soir, merci*' and wry smiles all round. Voluptuaries *manqués*, we turned our attention, if not our imagination, to art and the aesthetic treasures that Paris had to offer us.

On the *Quatorze Juillet* we crossed the city to the Place de la Bastille to join the procession chanting '*Libérez Thaelmann! Lib erez Thaelmann!*' We were in Europe and participating in the anti-Nazi struggle along with the French socialists and communists of the *Front Populaire*. Belfast and its Orangemen on parade to celebrate the victory at the Battle of the Boyne in 1690 seemed far away, remote in space and time, and we laughed at the

179

thought of the anachronistic parade at home compared to what was happening here. Here we were, in Paris, intoxicated after a few bocks, listening to the music from the cafés and the bands on parade, shaking hands with the French and shouting '*Bon santé*'. Paris was *en fête* and we were too.

From morning to evening we explored the city on foot, seldom boarding an *autobus* unless we found ourselves exhausted and miles away from Montmartre. Once, when I was tightly jammed against bodies on the rear platform of an *autobus*, I became aware of a young woman in a light dress swaying against me as the *autobus* swayed along the boulevard, and I could feel the contours of her warm body, from the back of her knees upwards, swaying as I swayed, her back turned to me so that I could see only her neck and shoulders and smell her perfume, her face all the while unseen so that I never learnt whether or not she was beautiful. All I was aware of was the mute yielding of her body as we moved together and then she suddenly moved away from me, jumped off the *autobus* and disappeared into the crowd on the pavement without looking back in my direction.

We learnt from the advertisements in *L'Humanité* that an International Congress of Writers against War and Fascism was to take place at the Mutualité with speeches by André Gide, Pablo Neruda, Heinrich Mann, E.M. Forster and others. We stood patiently in a queue until the doors opened, then suddenly our ranks were broken and everybody rushed forwards and I lost sight of Bob in the mêlée. Next to me a small elderly Frenchman with a drooping moustache became agitated and addressed me.

'*Où est ma femme? Monsieur, où est ma femme?*'

I hadn't noticed his wife disappearing in the scramble, so I shook my head and our neighbours did the same. He had lost his wife! Where had she gone? Could no one tell him? No one could. Then he cupped his hands round his mouth and called her name. No answering cry came from the lost one. What should he do? We were now near to the entrance and I thought it likely that Bob, by skilful use of his elbows, had pushed his way into the building before me. No need to worry about him, he was accustomed to edging his way through football crowds. But my French neighbour, now extremely agitated, had to decide whether to make his way into the building alone and hope to find his wife already there, or struggle clear of the mêlée and perhaps find his wife still outside waiting for him. Suddenly he shouted to all around him: '*J'ai perdu ma femme mais je ne perdrai pas ma place!*'

Though he had lost his wife he was determined not to miss the speeches in defence of democracy and freedom. His neighbours assured him that all would be well, but he cursed his fellow-countrymen for their lack of patience, their lack of courtesy to women, their lack of culture, accusing them of being as bad as the Nazis and the Fascists.

I'd no difficulty in finding Bob, who was waiting for me in the foyer, but my Frenchman, who was keeping close to me, looked round in vain for his wife. By now he was distressed and near to tears.

'*Quatre places!*' he declared triumphantly, putting his coat in one seat, his cap in another, and warning us not to allow anyone to take the two seats he'd grabbed for himself and his missing wife. And away he went in search of her, climbing up and down the aisles calling, '*Cécile! Cécile!*' At last a response came from the back of the gallery, where a small figure stood up gesticulating.

'*Ici! Ici! Ici!*'

And joyfully he trotted to the gallery to rescue her, his face radiant; and, linking her arm firmly for fear he might lose her again, he escorted her with marital possessiveness to her seat, with due acknowledgement to Bob and myself for our solicitude on his behalf.

'*Merci, messieurs. . . Merci, messieurs.*'

The congress opened; the famous European writers filed on to the platform to loud applause; and the speeches began.

The Palais de la Mutualité is a spacious hall and few writers are orators, so the Congress – as far as I was concerned – was something of a flop; and I can recall only the short-lived pleasure at seeing a phalanx of solemn literary figures on a platform and the boredom of listening to speeches in German, a language I didn't know; in French, a language I found difficult to follow; and in English, which I would have understood if only speakers – such as E.M. Forster – had used the microphones properly. So after a couple of hours Bob and I withdrew, having shaken hands with our elderly French couple whose enthusiasm for the proceedings exceeded ours. They told us they were Jewish, and their contretemps at the beginning of the Congress sticks in my memory as something endearingly human, while the speeches – which I read in *L'Humanité* the following day – have disappeared from my memory.

Still, for me, the occasion itself was memorable. It was the first Congress of Writers I ever attended and I haven't attended another since. All the same, I believe that there are times when writers should appear in public and declare where they stand on social issues; they are no more private or *au dessus de la bataille* than anybody else. And that year in Paris was certainly an occasion for writers to speak out against barbarism.

We made the obligatory trip to Shakespeare and Co., the small bookshop now in the Rue de L'Odéon which had published *Ulysses,* and we bought a copy to smuggle through the British Customs and exhibit at home as a trophy of our pilgrimage. Having purchased Joyce's masterpiece and a copy of *Transition,* we were brought into the little room at the back to inspect the lending library. There we spent half an hour chatting to the young American girl in charge of the shop, and displaying our knowledge of the writers whose photographs lined one of the walls – Joyce, Eliot, Pound, Lawrence, Scott Fitzgerald, Hemingway, Anderson and the others. Then when she asked us what our nationality was we declared that we were Irish, compatriots of Shaw and Synge and Yeats.

'Ah, that's why you are so interested in James Joyce! You are from Dublin?'

We shook our heads.

'From Belfast.'

Then we changed the subject and inquired whether Joyce ever came into the shop.

'Oh yes, he drops in from time to time.'

'Do you know when?'

But she couldn't tell us when, and Joyce didn't oblige us by calling in that afternoon.

We stayed about a fortnight in Paris, never leaving the city, not even for Versailles, before our money ran out. We lived cheaply, our only luxury an occasional bottle of wine. Paris is a city where it is always possible to live cheaply, and many of its greatest gifts are free. We swam in a Seine *piscine*, dawdled through the Louvre until our legs and eyes gave up, climbed the hill of Sacré Coeur for the view, attended Mass in Notre-Dame, marvelled at the Sainte-Chapelle, ate bread and cheese and drank our *vin rouge* on the Vert Galant while the river traffic glided by, took an *autobus* to Père-Lachaise to see Oscar Wilde's tomb and found it, but failed to find Héloïse and Abélard's and swore we'd return but didn't. We were disappointed by the Bois de Boulogne and spent a wasted afternoon there. I know it isn't easy to be bored in Paris but that hot and dusty afternoon we were bored and irritable. That was about all, except for the *bouquinistes* along the Seine and the bistros and the boulevards and the light and a couple of grey rainy days and the Jardin du Luxembourg, a happy place to be if you are happy yourself, sitting on a bench watching people pass and drinking your bottle of wine.

The English Channel was rough and I was sick all the way across, and even on the train as far as London. I slept most of the way to Liverpool, and there, on the boat, we heard the familiar Belfast accent and felt at home. And we almost were. No bunks in steerage, but no matter. We walked along the cold deck in the early morning before Donaghadee and Bangor came out of the mist. No one waiting on the dockside for us, and no money for a taxi; but we never took taxis anyway. Downstairs on a Cregagh tram and across the Albert Bridge. Belfast looked incredibly dull on a cloudy morning but it was home. We separated at Ravenhill Avenue, Bob going to the right towards Rosebery Road, and I to the left towards Loopland Road. Home again. Yes, home.

Once back home Bob and I longed to be away again, for Paris had unsettled us. Certainly I'd no intention of remaining in Belfast, so I applied for teaching jobs in England, France and Italy, but without success. In the meantime I had to be satisfied with the

Instruction Centre and the three pounds I collected every Friday. I comforted myself that at least I was working and contributing towards my keep. Father found it hard to believe that I had at last become a wage-earner who offered him two pounds every week. He'd been so accustomed to handing out money to me, week after week, year after year, that he couldn't get used to the new transaction. He always looked ill at ease when I put the money into his hand, and he accepted it reluctantly, or suggested a compromise.

'Ach, I hate takin' yer money, boy. But I suppose I should. It's right, isn't it?'

I assured him that it was.

'All the same, let's go halfers this week. That's fairer, isn't it?' And though I assured him that it wasn't, I often took ten shillings back to restore his feeling of what was right and proper.

'I've got to be tight-fisted wi' yer mother. But that doesn't mean I've got to be wi' you. Money's only money. An' too much of it is just as bad as too little. The trouble is, as you well know, it burns a hole in yer mother's pocket.'

Still he'd the consolation that mother was more stable than she used to be, but whether this would be permanent or whether she'd go off the rails again he couldn't be certain. There was no telling the ways of women in general, and he'd little faith left in mother. Still, according to the Bible, miracles did happen and I suspect that he often prayed for one to happen in our house. Father held on to his belief in prayer, and sometimes I'd see him kneeling at his bedside in his shirt, his head buried in his hands. Then with a sigh and his habitual gesture of straightening his unruly black hair he'd climb into bed and curl himself up as if thankful for the comfort and consolation of sleep.

I never once gave mother any share of my wages. This was the agreement that father and I had made, and I was ashamed of its meanness. And mother, though deceitful and unscrupulous in such matters with father, miraculously summoned up all her vestige of self-respect and never once begged me for money. It was a moral victory for her. She was well aware that in humiliating her I was also humiliating myself; and when the two of us were alone and I didn't speak, my thoughts bitterly resentful of what was happening to us, she'd break the silence: 'Yes, I know I've done bad things. I admit I have. But never forget I'm your mother, no matter what I've done or haven't done.' When mother said that I could have howled with anguish; instead I would sit perfectly still, staring at the wallpaper, my eyes swimming with tears. Then I'd leave the room, wishing I could embrace and comfort her, but unable to throw a kind word or look in her direction.

With grandma Leeman's death – which acted like a tonic on father's health, his step becoming springier and his skin clearer – mother settled into middle age and her drinking almost ceased; though now and again father confided in me that he suspected her breath smelt of alcohol. But, being unsure, he gave her the benefit of the doubt, knowing that if he challenged her she'd never admit guilt. So he let well alone, assuring me that at last he could see light at the end of the tunnel. Father used metaphors rarely, but when he did they were usually associated with the railway. 'When you drive an oul' engine too hard, something has to go bust' was one of his dicta, and another: 'There's no smoke wi'out fire, mind. Any driver'll tell you that.' And now father felt that we were 'on the upward grade', with my sister working as a shorthand-typist in Easons, and my brother attending the College of Technology.

Though I'd been glad to leave Chatsworth Street and Mount-pottinger school, I still continued to frequent Templemore Avenue library, which by now I felt almost belonged to me. One day, to my surprise, I was greeted by a new assistant called Cecil Harper who had been in my classes at Inst. At school we'd been acquaintances, but now we rapidly became friends. I've a lucky knack of finding friends at the right time, and the arrival of Cecil at what I considered to be my own library was but one instance of this serendipity. Brought up in what seemed to me an enormous villa in Ardenlee Avenue, Cecil had been only moderately successful at Inst. He had left a year before me to enter business as a window-dresser, a job that I would have rejected as beneath my dignity. The only explanation I could imagine for Cecil's bizarre choice was that his father owned a large sports shop in the centre of Belfast and that Cecil would eventually be taken into the family business. If this happened, window-dressing would be a useful skill for him to have. But, for some reason, this didn't happen. Instead Cecil joined the public library as an assistant, though he'd little taste himself for reading. Tall, flaxen-haired and freckled, he was extremely likeable and helpful; and sometimes I collected library books at his home not only because it was more convenient for me, but because if his younger sister, as flaxen-haired as himself, opened the door she would invite me into the large drawing-room and we'd chat until Cecil made his appearance. Though I was too diffident to confess my interest in her, I inquired from Cecil, as subtly as I could, how his sister spent her spare time, and was abashed to be told that she was about to be engaged. So that was that. The only consolation I got was when he added that his older sister was easily the most intelligent member of the family and had a degree in modern languages; but if that was a hint – and I'm not sure it was – I didn't take it. The older sister – dark and thin and about thirty – struck me as being devoted to teaching and committed to spinsterdom. It seemed to me, as far as women were concerned, literature was more rewarding than real life; less time was squandered on the unwilling and half-willing, and the beloved always proved to be more compliant:

La très-chère était nue, et, connaissant mon coeur,
Elle n'avait gardé que ses bijoux sonores. . .

It was with Cecil that I shared an incident one Saturday after he'd shown me round the stacks of the reference library in Royal Avenue. We were standing on the pavement when a Protestant flute band marched along Royal Avenue and headed for York Street.

'Let's follow it!' I suggested.

'Why?'

'To see what happens.'

'Are you daft or what?'

Despite my daftness Cecil accompanied me, swearing that if anything looked like happening he'd make himself scarce.

A couple of policemen walked alongside the band which struck up 'On the Green Grassy Slopes of the Boyne' as soon as it entered

York Street. About a dozen followers were dancing behind, with arms waving and voices bawling out the words of the tune. Then the two policemen ran in front of the band as it was passing the Co-operative shop. The band leader raised his silvery tasselled pole and the music ceased. An argument began and voices were raised.

'What's up?' someone asked a drummer.

'The polis is interferin'.'

'What for?'

'We're not allowed up York Street.'

'Why not?'

'The polis say we're not allowed to march in this area.'

'Why not?'

'They've got orders. We're not to annoy the Catholics!'

'Protestants can parade where they like!'

'Bloody idjits, them bobbies!'

'Don't break ranks, fellas!'

'Not an inch!'

'Houl on a minit, lads!'

The band slowly broke ranks during the hubbub and retreated as far as the pavement, leaving the two policemen in command of the street. Then the policemen also retreated to the pavement. The members of the band huddled together arguing among themselves. Cecil wanted to leave, I wanted to stay, curious to see what would happen next. Suddenly the band left the pavement, re-formed ranks, defiantly struck up 'The Green Grassy Slopes of the Boyne' again and proceeded along the street, their followers singing and dancing. The policemen retreated once again, having tried to do their duty.

'Cheerio,' Cecil called, waving his hand as he departed. I followed the band up York Street but prudently crossed to the docks side. I was eager for experience but not to the point of foolhardiness.

Half way along the street the band halted and the followers scattered, some crossing to the docks side. The band finished their tune before breaking ranks and returning to the pavement. I was wondering what was happening when somebody said they thought they heard a shot.

'Did you hear anythin', mister?'

'No,' I replied.

A couple of shots rang out as I answered and I ran into the hallway of a draper's shop. Three women joined me, all with shopping baskets, all middle-aged and breathless.

'This is a quare carry-on, mister. What are they shootin' at?'

'I don't know.'

'It's that bloody oul' band.'

'Ach, they'll do no harm if nobody pays attention t' them. They've nothin' better t' do.'

'They're only makin' trouble, aren't they?'

'A flute band can do no harm if nobody. . .'

'But why create a disturbance?'

I leant out of the hallway and noticed that the side window of the shop had been shattered. Two young women were tugging energetically at the bright-coloured dresses on display, before bundling them up their skirts, their figures suddenly grotesquely inflated. When one of the middle-aged woman caught sight of the two figures in flight, she pointed an accusing finger at them.

'Luk at them two hussies! Did ye see them? Lootin' the shop! Them boul heelers'll end up in prison!'

By now York Street was deserted. More shots rang out but where they came from we couldn't say. Outside the shattered window lay two odd shoes. On the other side of the street three men, each carrying a bulky brown-papered parcel, walked slowly in Indian file towards the Northern Counties station.

'Where's them fellas goin'?'

'They must be aff a boat!'

'Sailors?'

'Ay, foreigners. Lascars mebbe. God help them!'

If the three sailors heard the shooting they ignored it. Then after about a quarter of an hour people began to leave the doorways and hurried along the street. All was well again. No one was killed or wounded. The only damage was a few shattered shop windows and there had been a little private looting. Otherwise the city was peaceful.

When I next met Cecil and told him what had happened after he'd left me, he shrugged as if to say that such an incident was hardly worth mentioning.

'Stupid, isn't it?' was his only comment on the shooting.

I could hardly contradict him, but couldn't help thinking how Bob and I would have discussed the incident for hours, drawing all sorts of conclusions from it: how it derived from the historical and religious differences between the workers; how these riots were confined to the working-class areas; how the talents of the workers for music and the arts emerged in one form or another – flute bands, ballads, wall paintings and choirs. Curious how different my two friends were: Bob so gregarious and intense, Cecil so individualistic and laconic. Yet both were as restless and dissatisfied with their lives as I was with mine. Bob had no intention of spending his whole life in business. Chocolates were a luxury and the industry, despite its English paternalism, was based on the exploitation of African cocoa growers; in his view even the Quakers were entangled with imperialism. Cecil took not the slightest interest in all this but only wanted to find a job that would suit his own temperament; and when library work bored him he became an assistant manager in the Classic cinema. Later he emigrated to Canada to manage a cinema and I lost touch with him. Bob remained my friend for life. He had, I think, the right kind of discontent.

As the gulf between what my life might be and what it was became narrower, I began to feel better equipped to face the immediate future. I had no longer any strong desire to flee from Belfast and make a fresh start abroad. The romanticism that had propelled me to Rugby had disappeared. The reality was at home, and I'd have to face it as best I could.

Now I'd a back bedroom for a retreat, with a bookshelf, table and chair of my own. My job in the Juvenile Instruction Centre had proved to father that my studies hadn't been in vain, and though neither of us ever mentioned the financial support he had given me since I'd left Mountpottinger school until the day of my graduation ten years later, it was as if we had a pact between us never to forget it and to acknowledge it by our silence. That seemed right to both of us. As for mother, she'd never questioned my ability to become a teacher or anything else I put my mind to, and put all father's doubts down to what she regarded as his enormous ignorance of life outside the confines of the Belfast and County Down railway. So when I announced that I'd been given an MA for my thesis mother displayed no surprise at all and blithely remarked, 'Well, I knew you wouldn't find that very difficult.' Father, for his part, contented himself with the briefest of congratulations: 'That's good. Now, what next?'

I explained that my next move would be a change of job: two years of teaching in the 'Buroo School' was more than enough and H.O. White was urging me towards a career in extra-mural lecturing. He had already arranged for me to give a course of ten lectures on Anglo-Irish literature to an adult class, and nearly a hundred students had applied for places.

'Are ye bein' wise, boy, tryin' to fly as high as that?'

'I don't know.'

'If you're not sure then you'd be best to renege. That is, if it's not too late now. Couldn't you tell your friend Mr White. . .'

Father's lack of confidence not only in himself but in me always infuriated mother.

'You haven't the spunk yourself, Bob, to talk to anybody educated – you're that nervous you're afraid to open your mouth in front of them.'

'Oh, I haven't got your gift o' the gab, girl, an' mebbe it's just as well. It's got you into trouble more nor once before the day.'

It seemed to me that just as mother's love of company could lead her into all sorts of trouble – she'd even dabbled in spiritualism for a while – my own eagerness to grab as much education as possible could also land me into trouble. My course on Anglo-Irish literature, for example, wasn't as innocuous as I'd originally thought it might be. I was more interested in literature than in politics, but it soon became apparent that my class was more interested in politics than in literature. The result was that no matter what the subject might be – and the course ranged extravagantly and absurdly from Kuno Meyer's translations of

190

ancient Irish poetry to James Joyce's *Ulysses* – the discussion after each lecture was largely devoted to the national question and how Ireland might become united. That suited me well enough provided the discussions didn't end in bawling and fisticuffs, and they didn't; so I delivered my carefully composed lectures on Maria Edgeworth and William Carleton, James Clarence Mangan and George Moore to my politely attentive audience for the customary hour, waited politely for the relevant questions which too seldom came; then contended myself with the role of chairman of a lively political debating society.

When I reported to H.O. the waywardness of my students – almost all of them older than myself – he raised both hands in mock or mild disapproval, for I couldn't decide which, and twirled his wrists in a gesture indicative of his confusion. Even adult classes had to be subjected to some form of academic discipline and shouldn't be allowed to wander too far from the immediate topic. Surely I agreed?

'The secret is to guide and control your students. A loose rein but a firm one. Ah, but all that will come with experience!'

'But I couldn't keep politics out of my lectures, could I?'

'Of course not, of course not, dear fellow! But literature comes first, doesn't it? Else they've joined the wrong class. And tell them that!'

'I quoted Yeats's "Easter 1916".'

H.O. took a sharp intake of breath and made his gesture of playing a celestial harp.

'Magnificent poem! One of W.B.'s greatest. But we both know it can't be recited everywhere in Belfast. So take care. . .'

Grateful though I was for H.O.'s cautionary guidance, I'd no intention of following it. I'd more than my share of youthful arrogance and independence but enough commonsense and good manners not to risk losing his friendship.

But perhaps 'friendship' is too strong a word for a relationship almost devoid of emotion. Indeed H.O. appeared to me as a slightly eccentric middle-aged bachelor who enjoyed the company of young men and women but whose feelings towards them were entirely avuncular: almost a Henry James figure, sympathetic and serene, genteel and virginal; an academic and minor man of letters who lived his life between his study full of books and his lecture-room where he happily – and on occasion passionately – discoursed on books. H.O. loved talk and talked well, though like most good talkers he could be a monologuist, especially when addressing the young over a cup of tea. When we'd met in his study at the time I was determined to leave the university without finishing my degree he'd persuaded me to stay on, and afterwards he'd supervised my MA. Now he was urging me towards an academic career. Couldn't I proceed to Paris as he himself had done as a young man? He knew I was attracted to France and to French literature and saw no reason why I shouldn't live abroad for a year or two. He told me I should make up my mind and go.

But now it was impossible for me to do as he suggested. I had to go my own way.